CADOGAN CHESS BOOKS

Easy Guide to Chess

CADOGAN CHESS SERIES

Chief Advisor: Garry Kasparov
Editor: Andrew Kinsman
Russian Series Editor: Ken Neat

Other titles of interest include:

LEV ALBURT
Test and Improve Your Chess

YURI AVERBAKH
Chess Endings: Essential Knowledge

JOSÉ CAPABLANCA
Chess Fundamentals

WILLIAM HARTSTON
How to Cheat at Chess

JULIAN HODGSON
Chess Travellers Quiz Book

DANIEL KING
How Good is Your Chess?

STEWART REUBEN
Chess Openings - Your Choice

VLADIMIR VUKOVIC
The Art of Attack in Chess

SIMON WEBB
Chess for Tigers

For a complete catalogue of CADOGAN CHESS books (which
includes the Pergamon Chess and Maxwell Macmillan Chess lists)
please write to: Cadogan Books plc, London House, Parkgate Road,
London SW11 4NQ.
Tel: (071) 738 1961 Fax: (071) 924 5491

Contents

Introduction

What sort of game is chess? Before I do anything else, let me dispel the idea that it is a game for the intellectual few, beyond the powers of the average person. The chess of a 'master' may be; but so is the singing of a Caruso, the football game of a Pele... You can still derive immense pleasure from playing a game badly!

However, nobody really enjoys playing any game badly for year after year; there is a peculiar enjoyment in beating people who used to beat you, and the aim of this little book is to show you not only how chess is played but also how it can be played well. I have tried to provide you with the joys of improvement in the easiest way possible. I have been to great pains to condense the experience of many years' play in many countries, into a small book. At the same time I have not avoided repetitions and I have not shirked any detailed explanation because I want you to read, not with desperate concentration, but in the same lazy way as you read a novel or a newspaper. I am hoping this book will enable you to pick up chess easily, almost casually but correctly.

Chess is unique in so many ways that I can hardly spare space to recount them. What other game can you play by post with an opponent in, say, Australia? Or by telephone with an opponent maybe five thousand miles away - yet finish a game in an afternoon? It is the most international of all games, beating even tennis in this respect; it numbers its devotees in every civilised country - in Siberia, Mexico, India; Cape Town and Calcutta, Vancouver and Vladivostok. The Icelanders, a thousand miles North of Europe, are fine players. So are the Brazilians on the Equator. A man once wrote to me stating that he had found natives playing chess in the uncharted wilds of Central Madagascar, 'miles from anywhere'.

It must be one of the cheapest games. A chess club needs no field or pavilion, dressing room, goal posts; the player himself requires no special clothing, bat, racquet, cap or the like. Apart from a room, a few tables, light and heat - things which at a pinch, could easily be supplied by one of the members in his own house - a chess club need go to no further expense than a few cheap sets and boards. Anything more is a mere luxury. Except perhaps, a few chess clocks.

Another unique feature: the leading chess players (or 'masters' as they are nobly named) have a bigger public than leaders in any other pastime - this may make football fanatics gasp, but it is perfectly true. Games played between leading masters are recorded and reproduced in magazines and newspapers all over the world. Any unusually brilliant game is quoted from one to another, to be played over by millions of readers and bring its winner fame, not only in his own country, but abroad; not only in his own time but maybe for decades to follow.

What other kind of game can you play, if necessary, without a scrap of apparatus of any kind? Even noughts and crosses needs pencil and paper. 'Blindfold chess' is a development of the game by no means so uncanny, or even difficult, as most people imagine. The two participants picture board and men in their minds' eyes, calling out their moves in turn and keeping the positions in their heads throughout. It is not always the strongest players who are best at blindfold chess - quite mediocre players often have an almost instinctive capacity to retain the ever-changing positions in their imaginations, and occasionally a beginner takes to blindfold chess like a duck to water.

Unique is the literature of chess. More books have been written about chess than about any other game known, among them the second book ever printed in the English language.

There is one consideration which must mean something to every newcomer to the game. A tennis player is old at 40, a footballer at 35, a baseball 'babe' at 30, a table-tennis champion (they say) at 27. What satisfaction is there in finding your powers starting to wane almost before you have really mastered a game? What is there but disappointments and regret? At chess you can continue to consolidate and improve for a long, long time. Steinitz was still only a middle class player at 25, but he subsequently became World Champion and retained this title for over quarter of a century. Lasker, who succeeded him, was still playing well in master-tournaments at the age of seventy. Chess is a game of the mind, and mental powers continue to develop for longer than physical.

Again, as chess has no physical basis, it is possible to eradicate faults of style by diligent study, whereas in, say, tennis, a bad style picked up in your youth, when you could not afford expensive coaching, might hamper you for the rest of your life.

So from this book you can learn a game which can continue to provide you with interest an enjoyment, not for ten years or for twenty years, but till the end of your days.

1 The Men and their Moves

Chess is played on an ordinary draughts (checkers) board of sixty-four squares alternately coloured light and dark. The colours can actually be any two contrasting shades but are invariably called 'White' and 'Black' in discussion. As in draughts, the two players 'move' alternately from beginning to end. All the squares are used and the board must be placed so that each player has a white square in the corner nearest his right hand. ('White on your right' is easy to remember.) Look at any complete diagram in this book, and note that each player has a white square nearest to him at his right hand. Each player starts with sixteen men which are not all alike as in draughts but have varying powers. One can move in a certain way, another in another, and so on. Chess has many analogies with war and, when playing it, you can easily imagine yourself as a war Minister with various forces under your command, each with its own strengths and limitations; for instance your infantry moves slowly but can cross any sort of ground; your tanks can cross rough ground but are stopped by rivers; your navy is powerful at sea but useless on land, and so on. In chess, one of the men (the bishop) can move any distance diagonally, but not otherwise, whereas another, the king, can move in any direction, but only one square at a time; and so on.

Your only real task, in the beginning, is that of learning what each kind of chess man can and cannot do and, since there are only six different kinds of men all told, it is not difficult. In fact, you hardly need to learn, any more than you have had to 'learn' the meanings of thousands of different words you use in conversation every day. You play a few games - make a few mistakes like a child in its talk - but soon find that you know how each piece moves without bothering to think about it.

Checkmate

Each player has one man called a 'king'. The whole aim of chess is to corner your opponent's king.

We say 'checkmate' it, or practically always, for short, 'mate' it. You have mated your opponent's king and therefore won the game, when you are threatening to 'take' it and your opponent cannot do anything to prevent you.

As soon as you have subjected your opponent to this indignity, the game is over. This is all you are really playing for, from beginning to end - *don't forget!* The whole aim of the game is to get one particular man out of the sixteen your opponent starts the game with, namely his king, into your power.

You can capture your opponent's other men and remove them from the board, rather as in draughts. This usually helps, of course, but you must never become so interested in the process that you forget the real aim of the game.

To 'take' or 'capture' at chess, you lift the captured man off the board and place the capturing man on the square it occupied. Your own man throws out his adversary and grabs his bit of territory. You are not compelled to capture whenever you can, nor, naturally, is your opponent (this is a big difference from draughts, as also is the fact that you *never* jump over an enemy man). When a man is so placed that it could be captured, it is said to be *en prise* (pronounced 'on preez'); a man may often be left *en prise* for ten or twenty moves and then move away in the end without being captured at all.

There are various patterns of chessmen in use but none so popular or as pleasant to play with as the 'Staunton', so I hope, for your sake, that you have acquired a set of these; and I assume you have got them by you. Examine them.

Note that sixteen are white and sixteen black; these are the two opposing armies, one player taking command of the white men and the other of the black. 'White' makes a move first, then 'Black', then White again and so on in strict alternation until the game is over.

Each set of sixteen similarly coloured men comprises eight little ones, all alike, called pawns, and eight larger ones, of varying design, called pieces.

The two white pieces and the two black pieces which look like the castles were actually called 'castles' a century ago but we have reverted to an old name derived from the Persian, 'rooks'. These are powerful pieces, which can move any distance upwards, downwards, or sideways, but not diagonally. They act, in other words, along the 'ranks' and 'files', the ranks being the rows of squares across the board from side to side, and the files the rows at right angles to these, crossing the board from one player to another.

In printed diagrams, rooks are

shown like this:

White rook: ♖

Black rook: ♜

Next pick out the two pieces, one white, one black, which have a scalloped collar round their necks. These are the queens.

White queen: ♕

Black queen: ♛

The queen is the most powerful piece on the board. It can move any distance horizontally, vertically or diagonally; that is to say, along a rank, file or diagonal.

The pawns are easy to find. They are printed in diagrams like this:

White pawn: ♙

Black pawn: ♟

Each player has eight pawns. Their normal move is one square straight forward but they capture one square diagonally forward. They cannot move backwards but have one tremendous power which is, that whenever one reaches the opposite edge of the board unscathed, it can (actually must) be exchanged into any other man (except a king) its owner chooses. As the queen is the most powerful piece, the successful pawn is usually 'promoted' to a queen and we then say the pawn has been 'queened'. It doesn't matter if the player's original queen is still on the board; he can acquire a second queen, and even a third or fourth, if he is so lucky.

The Knight's Move

The next piece we come to is the knight, also easily recognised, for both the piece and the printed symbol for it (which we give herewith) bear a horse's head:

White knight: ♘

Black knight: ♞

It has a rather peculiar move which some people grasp at once but which bothers others. In case you find it hard, I shall explain it carefully.

Look at Diagram 1. The knight there could move at choice to any of the eight squares marked with an 'X'. If an enemy piece or pawn stood on any of those squares, the knight could capture it *(in all chess diagrams White goes up the board).*

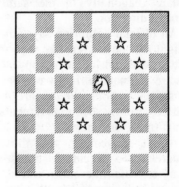

Diagram 1

I have come across four different definitions of the knight's move and I am going to give all four. Whatever you do, don't try to memorise them all. Read them carefully, make up your mind which seems the clearest to you (it is curious how tastes differ), make a note of it and forget the rest.

i) A knight moves to the next-but-one square of opposite colour to the square on which it stands. It moves from a white square to a black square, or from a black to a white, never from white to white or from black to black. Verify this from the diagram.

ii) It moves two squares in one direction, then one at right angles. You may find it easier to understand the knight's move if you picture it as taking place in a little box of six squares, which it crosses from corner to corner.

iii) It moves one square forwards or sideways and then one square diagonally in the same general direction.

An official definition says 'the knight can be moved like a rook one square and like a bishop one square, the square finally reached must not adjoin the square it started from, such movements constituting one move'.

iv) It moves to just those squares two squares' breadth away to which the queen can *not* move. You remember that the queen can move any distance up, down, or diagonally? In other words, the queen can move any distance North, South, East or West; or NE, NW, SE, or SW. The knight can move to any of the eight intermediate compass points NNE, NNW, ENE, etc., etc., not 'any' distance but just two squares.

Imagine the knight in Diagram 1 replaced by a queen. The queen could move to any destination not more than two squares away except those to which the knight could move (and which we have marked by 'X's). This property of the knight is useful; it is the only man which can attack the queen without being attacked by the queen in return.

Read over each of these four explanations, consulting Diagram 1 each time, and confirming that they all describe the knight's moves and that each of the knight's moves illustrated on the diagram conforms to them. Then decide which explanation you find easiest and - forget the others, or they will only muddle you!

We have now picked out of our set of chessmen the queens, the kings, the pawns, the rooks, the knights and there should be only four pieces left, two black, two white. These are the bishops. The top is supposed to represent a bishop's mitre.

White bishop: ♗
Black bishop: ♝

As we have already mentioned, the bishop moves diagonally, so that the powerful queen combines the moves of a bishop and rook, being able to move like either at choice. There is nothing more deadly than a queen in full flight!

Capturing

Diagram 2

Diagram 2 shows the capture of a black bishop by a white rook. White plays his rook onto the square occupied by the bishop and removes the latter from the board.

It surprises beginners to learn that, among the masters, the knight is considered the weakest of the pieces, mainly because of the shortness of its range: a queen, rook or bishop can cross the board in a single move, whereas a knight cannot do it in fewer than three.

To beginners its strangeness overweighs every other consideration, so it is worthwhile making an effort to familiarise yourself with its move at the very beginning for, in doing so, you will be immediately ensuring yourself a big advantage over many fellow students who go in abject fear of its vagaries for months. The sooner you relegate the knight to its rightful place as a useful but far from terrifying piece, the more quickly you will become a good player.

You will already have gathered that the king is a rather peculiar piece since the fate of the whole 'side' depends on him. You have already learnt his move, one square in any direction. Naturally this means he cannot move like a knight, for you cannot move *one* square NNE, or you would not finish up in the middle of a square. He can move to any of the eight squares next to him.

White king: ♔

Black king: ♚

You may be unlucky and have got hold of a second-hand set in which the cross has been knocked off the top of his crown. The king's cross seems to be the most vulnerable part of a chess set and, at a rough estimate, I should say that twenty percent of the sets in use have the crosses knocked off one or both of the kings!

Mainly owing to the fact that his being mated spells the end of the game, the king has various eccentricities. For instance he can never be captured; the kings remain on the board from the beginning to the end of the game. He can never be left in a position where he could be captured; i.e., if an enemy piece threatens him he must immediately get away from the attack. Every other plan must go by the board until his cry of distress has been heeded. Often the player making the move which attacks him says 'Check!' *A check is a threat to capture a king.* Any move which does not immediately attend to the check is illegal, cannot stand and can be punished.

There are three ways of getting out of any attack, and these, for a check, are:

(a) Capturing the attacking piece;

(b) Moving the king; or

(c) Interposing a piece between the attacking piece and the king.

Only when the check has come from a queen, bishop or rook is this last resource available; when the checker is a pawn or a knight, capturing it, or moving the king, are the only resources.

The king can never move into check, i.e. make a move which would allow an enemy piece to capture him in reply. Consequently, the two kings can never occupy adjacent squares, because the one could capture the other.

Some Illustrative Positions

In Diagram 3 the white rook is giving check, since it could capture the black king next move. It must now be Black's turn to move and he must attend to the check at once; by capturing the rook with the queen, or moving the queen in between the king and

the rook, or moving the king so that it is no longer in check.

Diagram 3

To move the king one square left would not avail, because it would leave him still subject to capture by the rook, i.e. still in check. Nor could he move the king one square towards the rook for the same reason. Nor could he move on to the black square in between him and the white king because there he would be in check from the latter. He could go to any of the marked squares, however, and then be out of check.

In Diagram 4 the black king can get out of check by moving on to any of the black squares next to him, or by capturing the bishop. He cannot move to the white square above him to his left because he would then be liable to capture by the bishop; nor to that below him on his left, because then he could be captured by the white king. He could move away to the North-east.

Diagram 4

Diagram 5

Here the black king is mated. The rook is attacking him, and prevents his escaping either East or West. The knight prevents his moving NE or NW and the bishop prevents his moving North or South. Finally, the white king prevents him from moving SW and the pawn from moving SE. He cannot capture the attacking rook so cannot escape in any way. Checkmate! White has won!

For some other checkmate positions turn to Chapter 3.

Limitations to Moves

It might have surprised you to learn how powerful the chessmen are. The bishop can travel *any distance* diagonally! A rook *any distance* vertically or horizontally. 'It's a wonder', murmurs a draughts player, 'there isn't an explosion!'

Of course every piece, at practically every stage of the game, is obstructed by other pieces. The fact that captures are not compulsory makes a lot of difference. 'Take it or leave it' is the slogan in chess. A piece or pawn may remain capturable but uncaptured for many moves if one player is satisfied all the time that it is best to leave it in that position, and the other that he gains nothing by capturing it.

Naturally a piece which is *en prise* (capturable) like this is usually 'protected' by some other man, i.e. another man of his own side is so stationed as to be able to recapture an enemy piece capturing him. The next diagram shows a knight 'protected' by a pawn. Naturally the knight is safe against capture by the black queen, for the pawn would immediately recapture and Black would have given away his powerful queen for a knight.

Diagram 6

A man can move on to a square occupied by a hostile piece, as we have seen, capturing it. Replace that hostile piece by another of his own colour: now he cannot move to that square. The friendly piece blocks his action or movement in that direction. Two men can never occupy the same square.

Diagram 7

A chessman cannot move *through* another. The knight may

appear to do this but such is not the case; its line of action runs between the immediately adjacent squares, so that it can pass between the bishop and rook in Diagram 7 to the square beyond.

Hence no other man can block a knight's move in any direction. If every unmarked square on Diagram 1 were occupied by other pieces, the knight would be able to move to any of the squares marked with an 'X'.

Let us take another position at random, to illustrate the powers of the pieces.

Diagram 8

In this position:

(a) The white rook could, at choice, move one square to the left; or two squares, or three squares or four, to the left; or one square down; or one square up; or two squares up or three squares up, in which last case he would capture the black bishop. These are the only moves legally available to the rook in this position,

He cannot move right at all, because the white pawn - a friendly piece - occupies the next square.

If he were to capture the bishop, he would give check to the black king and Black would have to get his king out of check before doing anything else.

(b) The knight could also capture the bishop; or it could move on to any of the black squares just above the black king; or to the square just in front of the rook, or to the black square on the right hand edge of the board and nearest the bottom. Not to any other square. It could have moved on to the square occupied by the white pawn if that had not been occupied by a friendly man.

(c) The white king can only move legally to one square, the white square to his North-west. On the right he is stopped by the edge of the board. If he were to move to either of the squares below him, he could be captured by the black king, so cannot legally move there at all. The other two black squares by him are similarly 'covered' and rendered uninhabitable to him by the black bishop.

(d) The black bishop can move to any of the thirteen squares on the two diagonals which intersect where he stands. Count up the squares for yourself, to confirm this.

(e) Where can the black king move? Not to any of the three squares just above him for they are all 'covered' by either the white king or the white knight. Five other squares are open to him, he could move one square right, left, down SW or SE. If he were to move one straight down, he would capture the white knight.

Bear in mind that: (a) pieces capture in the normal way of their moves; and that (b) men of the same colour obstruct one another.

Pawns

Pawns have several peculiarities - it is just like the little fellows to be awkward. To begin with, a pawn can't move backwards; it is the only man which cannot. Then, unlike any piece, it captures in a different way from its ordinary move. It *moves* straight forward but *captures* one square forward diagonally.

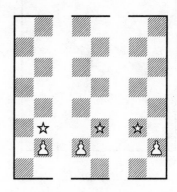

Diagram 9

The diagram shows the two

sorts of move. Have you got them? A pawn's normal move is one square *straight* forward; if it wants to make a capture, however, it can only do so if there is an enemy piece on one of two squares, of the same colour as that which he occupies and *diagonally* in front of him, in which case he jumps into the square occupied by that piece (or pawn), ejecting the latter.

If there is an enemy man on the square directly in front of him, then he cannot capture it - and he cannot move onto that square either, being blocked as effectively as if it were occupied by one of his own pieces. If there is an enemy piece on the square in front of him but no enemy piece on the square either side of it, then the pawn cannot move at all, as in the next diagram.

Diagram 10

The pawn cannot move or capture.

The next complication arose through impatience. People found it slow waiting for the pawns to come to grips with each other in the middle of the board at the beginning of the game, so they introduced a rule that a pawn should be able to move 'two' squares forward for this first move, if desired, instead of one. This applies, for any pawn to its *first* move only, note! The first move you make with any pawn can be one square forward or two squares forward, whichever you prefer; afterwards, that particular pawn may advance one square only at a time. You are never allowed to 'capture' two squares away, they have never altered the capturing rule, so that a pawn, whether on its first move or any other, can only capture one square away diagonally.

A final complication is the *en passant* rule, which we should discuss before moving any further.

The white pawn in the next diagram (No. 11) could be captured by the black one, if it were to move one square forward.

As it is on the square where it commenced the game, it could elect to jump two squares instead of one, and might thus evade this capture. The white pawn in Diagram 12 might become a passed pawn at a bound, jumping to the square between the two black ones. In situations such as these, a special rule gives Black the right to capture the pawn as if it had advanced only one square, instead of the optional two.

Diagram 11

Diagram 12

In making the capture, he plays his pawn on to the square which the white pawn would have occupied had it advanced only one square (in each of these two diagrams, the white square in front of the white pawn). Black must make the capture *at once* or he loses the right to do so; if he should make any other move in reply to White's double pawn

advance, he would lose for the rest of that game the right to capture that particular pawn of yours with that pawn of his.

In Diagram 12, either of the black pawns could make the *en passant* capture.

Diagrams 13 and 14 show positions before and after a typical *en passant* capture, from Diagram 11. Diagram 13 shows the position after White's move and Diagram 14 after Black's reply, capturing *en passant*.

Diagram 13

Diagram 14

It looks curious to capture in this way a pawn which had tried to jump past you, moving your pawn into an empty square, and removing one of your opponent's pawns from another square. It is easiest to remember like this: for one move, you have the right to act as if your opponent's pawn had advanced only one square instead of two.

This is called capturing *en passant* (meaning 'in passing'), a title which explains itself. Only a pawn has power to capture *en passant*; the pawn in the next diagram could be captured by the bishop if it were to advance one square; if it were to make a double jump, the bishop could only look on helplessly, for he has no power to capture *en passant*, and the pawn would have eluded him.

Only on a pawn's first move can it be captured *en passant* - naturally, since at no other time can it advance two squares at once. To be able to capture *en passant*, a pawn must stand on its possessor's fifth rank.

It would be neater, I suppose, if odd rules like this and castling, were eliminated and every man in chess had only one sort of move from beginning to end of the game, but centuries of trial have evolved the game as we know it today and as every innovation was ultimately tested from the view point: 'Does it make the game more enjoyable?' we cannot complain.

Diagram 15

Draws

As we have seen, a game of chess can be won by a checkmate. People often resign, to save time, when they see there is no hope of avoiding an ultimate checkmate.

A game is drawn:

(a) When a player is not able to make any legal move *but* his king is not in check. This is called 'stalemate' and examples are given in Diagrams 29 and 30. If the king of a player who is 'stalemated' were in check, he would be checkmated, so that this form of draw is often hailed with a gasp of relief;

(b) If the same position, with the same player to move, occurs three times and a correct claim is made by that player;

(c) If 50 successive moves on each side are made without a capture or a pawn move;

(d) If at any stage the two

players agree to call it a draw;

(e) If one player can submit the other to an endless series of checks ('Perpetual check').

A common perpetual check position is shown in Diagram 16.

ing to and from the square marked 'X'; you will find that the white king has no choice but to move to and from the white square to his right.

Ranks, Files and Diagonals

A rank is a straight row of squares across the board. This is White's first rank:

Diagram 16

Here the queen can deliver an endless succession of checks by oscillating between her present square and the white square at the lower right-hand corner.

Diagram 18

This is White's second rank:

Diagram 17
In Diagram 17, the black queen similarly forces a draw by mov-

Diagram 19

Diagram 20 shows White's eighth rank (and it is of course at the same time, Black's *first* rank). It is the 'opposite edge of the board' which we referred to on page 11; it is when one of White's pawns reaches a square in this rank that it can be 'queened' or otherwise promoted.

Diagram 20

A file is a straight row of squares up the board from one player to his opponent (see Diagram 21).

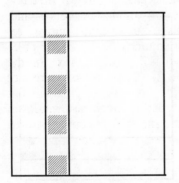

Diagram 21

A diagonal is a straight row of squares, all black or all white, touching at the corners only, as shown in Diagram 22. These terms rank, file and diagonal are very useful in discussion.

Diagram 22

A Final 'Once Over'

You should be quite familiar with the moves of the pieces by now, but just in case you are not, I suggest you re-read this chapter carefully before moving on to the rest of the book.

Don't forget the great aim of the game, *not* to capture your opponent's men but to mate his king. 'Get that man!'

All this may have sounded somewhat bewildering but when you have once grasped this first chapter, you have grasped all the real essentials. From now on, you can begin to enjoy yourself.

2 Starting and Finishing the Game

To start a game, the men are placed like this:

Diagram 23

The pieces (i.e. all the men but the pawns) are placed in a definite order along each player's back rank; the pawns occupy the two rows or ranks in front of them which, incidentally, we call the 'second ranks'. Among the pieces, the rooks occupy the outermost positions; then, coming inward from either right or left, we have in turn knights, bishops, king and queen. The kings face each other across the board, the queens likewise; the black queen goes on a black square, the white queen on a white square.

Even nowadays, a chess set arranged ready for play is an attractive sight. It must have looked even more stirring a thousand years ago, when the two sets were often elaborately carved. A king was a much more important personage in the old days - if he should happen to be bad-tempered, it might affect thousands of his subjects; that is probably why the custom arose of making his fate decide the conflict in chess. The 'queen' used to be his Grand Vizier or Prime Minister before she somewhat unaccountably turned into a woman; which explains her power. The game passed through innumerable changes in the first few centuries of its existence and, whilst the queen's move remained much the same, the piece moving it changed sex. In the same way, the rooks were not castles at all originally, but howdahs on elephants, which, in Persia and India where chess was born, were fearsome adjuncts to warfare. In Russia, the bishops were ships for a while - which is highly logical if you reflect how a bishop normally gets up the board by 'tacking' like a ship advancing against the wind. And so on. There is a story in every chessman. It is said that the game was invented as a substitute for war, providing a contest with all the thrills of warfare and many of the ideas and stratagems, but none of the bloodshed and misery.

Castling

In the early history of chess, people often found it risky to leave the kings on their original squares, so kept shuffling them away to the right or left as soon as neighbouring pieces had been moved. Also they found that the rooks, to be properly utilised, had frequently to be brought to the middle of the back row where the king and queen originally stood; so that in game after game each player would waste perhaps six or seven moves exchanging the positions of his king and a rook. To speed up the game, a special move was introduced by which the interchange could be considerably speeded up. You remember they used to call rooks 'castles'? They call this special move 'castling' to this day. It brings a rook into play and takes away the king into safety.

The king can 'castle' either to right or to left, collaborating with whichever rook lies on the side he moves to, and this is how it is done:

The king moves two squares towards the chosen rook, and the rook is then placed on the square over which he has passed.

The king is further from one rook than the other; this does not affect the above rule, which covers both cases, but it does affect the final position reached. The diagrams show the state of affairs after castling, in each case.

(a) With the nearer rook:

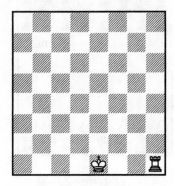

Diagram 24
Before castling kingside

Diagram 25
After castling kingside

(b) With the more distant rook:

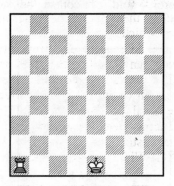

Diagram 26
Before castling queenside

Diagram 27
After castling queenside

Castling is illegal:

(a) If either the king or the rook has previously moved (even if they have subsequently moved back to their original squares);

(b) If the king is in check; you can never utilise castling to move out of check;

(c) If the square the king passes over, or the square it finishes on, is under attack from an enemy man; or

(d) If any square between the king and the rook is occupied.

Once you move your king you cannot 'castle' for the rest of that game; if you move one of your rooks, then you cannot castle with that rook, though you may with your other. Note that you can castle to save a 'rook' from attack; there is nothing illegal in castling when either the original square of the rook, or a square it passes over but which the king does not, is under hostile fire. Note also that, however many times a king has been checked, if he has never *moved* to escape the check, he has still the right to castle.

Mate Positions

Now you know how to set up the pieces for the game, how they move and capture and what you must strive for. I need only point out a few typical mating positions to save you from the annoyance of finishing several pieces to the good, yet being unable to effect a mate with them; and you will be ready for your first game.

In the positions which follow, the king mated is the black one.

A queen, aided by her king alone, can deliver mate. Manoeuvre the adverse king to the end of the board and then play the queen to the square in front of him, supported by your own king, as in Diagram 28, which should be carefully examined to verify that the black king is attacked where he stands and has no way of evading the attack.

Diagram 28

The queen *must* be supported! Take the white king away from this little part of the board, and Black has one heaven-sent resource: he cannot move to any unoccupied square by him, because these are all covered by the white queen, *but he can capture the queen herself.*

Watch Out for Stalemate!

When trying to mate your opponent with king and queen, guard carefully against the danger of stalemating him, as in Diagrams 29 and 30. If it is Black's turn to move here, the game is drawn by stalemate. Should Black have a pawn somewhere else on the

board which is free to move, there would of course be no stalemate.

Diagram 29

Diagram 30

As explained in Chapter 1, stalemate is a draw.

More Standard Mates

Another typical mate by the queen is shown in the next diagram.

Diagram 31

has drawbacks, as we shall see later.

Diagram 32

Here the white king covers the three squares in front of the black king, whilst the queen covers the three squares parallel to them in the rank he is on. A rook would serve for this mate just as well as the queen, since the queen's power along diagonals (which are all that a rook lacks in contrast to her) is not being used. In fact, this is the normal mating position finally reached, when mate has to be delivered by a rook alone.

Another common mate by a rook is shown below. Black has previously castled and played away both his rooks from the back rank, so that he is helpless against this sharp stab in the side. His own pawns prevent his escaping to any square on his second rank. It is occasionally useful to move one of these pawns at an early stage to provide an 'escape-hole' and prevent this sort of debacle; on the other hand, to break the line of your pawns in this way

Here is a mate which demonstrates the powers of the bishop and the knight. In this case they are again aided by black men robbing the king of two of his possible escape squares:

Diagram 33

And here is another fairly common combinative mate: The rook prevents the king from moving to the left or to the white square on the right, and attacks him where he stands; the bishop prevents the king from moving to the black square in front of him or (important!) capturing the rook.

Diagram 34

One bishop alone (assisted by the ubiquitous king) cannot deliver mate. Two bishops can, but only by driving the adverse king into a corner of the board, thus:

Diagram 35

The Queen's or Rook's Barrier

In all the mate positions given up to now, you may observe that the king mated has been driven to the edge of the board. It is naturally easier to administer the finishing touch when his escape in one or more directions is prevented by the edge of the board. Do not take this as meaning that the king is safer, as a general rule, in the centre of the board; he would often be at the mercy of hostile pieces there.

In striving for a mate, it is worth noting that a rook or a queen can set up a barrier to the passage of a hostile king which stretches right across an open board. Here the queen commands every square on the file (i.e. vertical row of squares) it stands on:

Diagram 36

Consequently, the black king could not move to any of the

squares on its left and is, indeed, confined to six squares along the right-hand edge of the board as long as the queen remains where she is. These are, the square he is on, and the five immediately below him. Replace the queen by a rook, and the king would still be confined to that file but he could now move one square upwards as well.

Incidentally, in a position such as Diagram 36, *don't* check with your queen by moving it to the edge of the board; this would let the black king out of his prison into the open board. Move up your white king as shown by the 'X'; Black cannot then escape being mated next move as in Diagram 28. Ignorance of this little principle may waste you much time at the end of a won game.

A bishop cannot set up a barrier like this:

Diagram 37

Here the black king can cross

the bishop's diagonal onto the white square to his North-west. *Two* bishops co-operating can form a barrier, thus in Diagram 35 no black king could cross the board from South-west to North-east, assuming the bishops avoid being captured. Try it!

You should soon learn how to deliver mate before exchanging down to such simple endings as these. Two or three pieces working together can make an enemy king uncomfortable, especially if some of the escape-squares in his immediate vicinity are blocked by his own men, as they will be for the major part of every game.

A Beautiful Mating Combination

Diagram 38 shows a beautiful though well known mate which illustrates this brilliantly. Start from this position, Black having obviously castled with the rook originally the closer to his king.

The white queen moves one square forward, 'check!' She cannot be captured now, but Black has two ways of evading the check. He can put the rook in between the queen and his king, but then the queen could capture it giving check again, and she could not be captured by the black king because that would be moving into check from the white knight. This continuation is bad, so Black will choose the other alternative and move his king into the corner.

Diagram 38

Now White moves his knight onto the square in front of the black rook; in doing so he threatens to capture the black king with it. 'Check!' again:

Diagram 39

Black can answer this check by (a) capturing the knight with the rook; or (b) bringing his king back again on to the white square to his left; as we have seen, 'in-terposing' to counter a check from a knight is never feasible. Of these alternatives the first is distasteful at first glance, for White, by recapturing the rook with his queen, would have gained a rook for a knight - a good bargain for him, a bad one for Black. (Actually, White has stronger replies still.) So Black moves the king back on to the white square; but now comes a catastrophe.

White moves his knight to the square in front of the white king. In doing so he delivers a double check - two checks at once! (Diagram 40).

Diagram 40

For both his king and his knight are threatening to capture the black king next move. The check from the queen is of a type known as the 'discovered check'; in giving it, the queen does not move herself but has her line of fire opened or cleared, as a result of a move by a friendly piece which previously obstructed it. Nowadays we should normally call this an 'uncovered' check, had not the term 'discovered' check been adopted centuries ago, and persisted.

Briefly, a 'discovered' check is the type given whenever the piece giving the check is *not* the piece moved.

Double Check

A discovered check is worse than an ordinary one as a rule, because the piece which clears itself out of the way to give the check can do all sorts of damage. It might make a capture, but can be immune from immediate recapture because the check from the other piece whose attack it uncovered has to be attended to first.

A double check is a check from two pieces at once. It is a discovered check, where the piece which moves, as well as the piece behind, gives check. This can be particularly horrible. Two of the usual resources for meeting a check are ruled out at once: you obviously cannot capture two pieces at the same time, nor can you interpose a piece so as to screen your king from two converging line of attack. So there is only one resource left - flight. *The only answer to a double check is a move of the attacked king.*

So here the hapless black king

must go back to his corner. If he were to move out to the only other square unobstructed by his own pieces, the white square in front of his rook, he would still be in check from both the queen and the knight.

Now White plays his queen onto the square the king has just vacated. Check again, and this time a check to which there is only one reply. There is no room for interposition. The king cannot capture the queen, for the square on which she stands is still commanded by the knight; nor can he move anywhere else. So the rook must capture the queen.

Now comes the climax. The knight moves so as to give mate, as depicted in Diagram 41.

Diagram 41

The black king is in check from the knight, which cannot be captured; and all the three squares to which he might move are blocked by his own pieces. This is aptly termed a 'smothered mate', the king being smothered by his own men, which block his escape.

If you study this little line of play carefully, you will set the seal on your knowledge of the moves of the pieces; you will have made acquaintance with two special kinds of check and obtained a glimpse of the beauty of chess. Noteworthy is the manner in which, just before the end, White deliberately gives up his queen for nothing, because he sees that he can force mate and thus win the game.

Now have a game with somebody! Preferably another learner. It won't be great chess but you'll enjoy it. On the other hand if you prefer to read on, you'll find the next chapter very instructive at this stage, for it deals with an interesting topic, the relative values of the various pieces and the pawns.

3 Values of the Men

Diagram 42

This diagram shows a ridiculous but not impossible position, which teaches an important lesson. White has lost all but two of the men with which he started; Black has not lost one. Yet the game is over, and White has won because the black king is mated!

We look on a queen as far more powerful than a rook, and a rook as far more powerful than a pawn and are justified in doing so in the vast majority of instances; but here Black has a queen, two rooks, two bishops, two knights and seven pawns more than his opponent yet has lost the game! The one white pawn is superior to

all of them. Why? Because it is supremely well placed, whereas all Black's men are very badly placed. Nothing could show more vividly that any estimate of relative strengths of the pieces must take the factor of position into account. Rarely indeed is the disparity so great as here, though often a player gives two or three pieces to give mate with the remainder of his force. In case you should regard the above position as too fantastic, however, here is the actual conclusion to a game between two leading Polish players some time ago:

Diagram 43

How many extra pieces does

White have? Four! Yet he has lost because his king is mated!

Although such violently paradoxical positions are rare, it is safe to say that the relative values of the pieces are influenced by their situations at every stage of every game. Here we may find a knight so well posted that it is as useful as a queen; there we may find a queen so badly placed that it is weaker than a bishop. An easily understandable case is that of a pawn, which can be promoted to a queen if it reaches the furthermost rank. With every square it advances, its chances of becoming a queen increase; and as these chances increase, so does its value to its possessor though to an extent sometimes difficult to gauge. If it is two squares from the 'queening' square and completely held up by enemy pieces, it may still be worth little more than when it started on its journey. If it has only one square to go and can hardly be hindered from advancing, it may be - for all practical purposes - worth a queen already.

It is thus quite misleading to calculate as if every piece retained the same unaltering value from the first move to the last, and to assume that the 'equations' I am going to give you are as reliable as 'twice five are ten'. Each represents a rough average of something which is constantly varying.

You will find the following little table very useful if you *never* forget this, and take the values as approximate and variable *averages* only:

Taking the value of
a pawn as 1 unit
a bishop or knight is worth 3 units
a rook is worth 4½ units
a queen is worth 9 units
To elaborate:

A rook is worth a bishop-and-a-half, or a knight-and-a-half; or a pawn-and-a-half more than either a knight or a bishop.

The Bishop

At first glance, there seems little to choose between a rook and a bishop. The former can move any distance along the rank or the file on whose junction it stands; the latter can move any distance along either of the two diagonals on whose junction it stands. We have already pointed out, however, that a rook can set up a 'barrier' across the board in the same way as the queen in Diagram 36, whereas a bishop can not. This often counts.

Furthermore, owing to the peculiar geometry of the chessboard, a rook commands more squares as a rule than a bishop. Place a rook and a bishop, in turn, on one of the central squares of the board. You will find that the rook could move, at choice, to any of fourteen different squares, whereas the bishop could only go to thirteen.

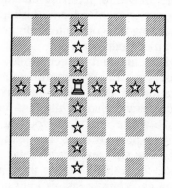

Diagram 44

Diagram 46

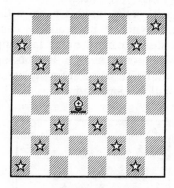

Diagram 45

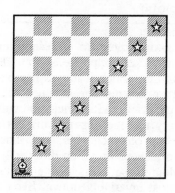

Diagram 47

Repeat the counts from some square nearer the edge of the board, and you will find the disparity is even greater. Place the pieces on corner squares, and you will find that the bishop's count has gone down to seven, whereas the rook's remains at fourteen.

Obviously the number of squares it can keep under its eye at any time is a good measure of the value of a piece; we see that a bishop is inferior to a rook in this.

We have not yet mentioned the bishop's chief weakness, which is that, owing to the nature of its move (diagonal), it is confined to squares on one colour from beginning to end of a game. Starting on a white square and moving diagonally, it can never get onto a black square, however much it twists and turns. As long as a player retains both his bishops, this weakness is not too keenly felt; but as soon as one of them is exchanged off, it may become so. Suppose your white-square bishop has been exchanged off; your opponent need only move his men onto white squares to make your remaining bishop almost useless.

'Bishops of Opposite Colour'

This weakness of a bishop on squares of opposite colour to those on which it moves has one rather striking consequence. If a game draws to its conclusion with every piece exchanged off but a bishop on each side, and those two bishops move on differently-coloured squares, the game is almost invariably drawn. Even if one player has a pawn, or even two pawns more than his opponent, he may be unable to win. Neither player can achieve anything. One is all-powerful on the white squares but weak on the black, the other *vice-versa*. Hence the first will always find it highly dangerous, perhaps impossible without loss, to advance any of his men onto a black square, so that they all become stuck on white; and his opponent will similarly be stuck on black. Listening to the conversation of keen players, you will often hear them refer to *bishops of opposite colour*; they are referring to this phenomenon of adverse bishops operating on opposite coloured *squares* producing a draw.

The diagram which follows provides a little practical demonstration of this. Black has five more pawns than White but, unless White blunders foolishly, cannot possibly win. Try it out; take one side and get a friend to take the other. Verify that, as long as White keeps his king unmoved and his bishop on the long diagonal it at present occupies, Black cannot move a pawn without having it immediately captured. He cannot move his king so can only shuffle his bishop about helplessly and finally agree to call the game a draw.

Diagram 48

Other instances of the bishop's weakness on squares of the other colour are given later.

So much for the bishop.

The Knight

A knight is inferior to a rook mainly in the shortness of its stride; as we have seen, it needs at least three moves to cross a board, whereas a rook can do it in one. In the middle of an open board, a knight commands eight squares (e.g. those marked with stars in Diagram 1). Move him to the side of the board, as in the next diagram, and he commands four; move him to the corner as in Diagram 50, and he commands only two. These figures compare badly with the bishop's, and worse with the rook's proud total of fourteen squares from anywhere on the board. A knight suffers from the cramping action of the edges of the board in a way that is out of all proportion, so that, more than any other piece, he should be kept near to the centre.

Diagram 50

A knight has two elements of strength. Its line of action cannot be blocked by any other man, either friendly or hostile (Diagram 7), so that, as we have seen, a check from a knight cannot be answered by interposition.

For the same reason, a knight can be very useful when a position is 'blocked' as shown in Diagram 51.

Diagram 49

Diagram 51

It is the situation of the pawns which determines whether or not a position is 'blocked'; since pawns can only move straight forward except when capturing, they can jam each others' progress and become so immobile that they reduce the mobility of the pieces too. In Diagram 51, how are the white pieces to get at the black, or the black to get at the white? In such a position as this, knights achieve more than other pieces, because they can infiltrate among the pawns where the others cannot.

On the other hand, when most of the pawns have been exchanged off, or when they are scattered about so freely as to not affect the mobility of the pieces, the knights are of little use due to the shortness of their stride. They may be late arriving on the scene at a critical moment as a result.

As we have seen, a knight moves from a white square to a black, or *vice versa*, never from a white square to a white. As a result of this he can never 'save' or 'lose' a move: if he could get to a particular square in one move, he could get to it in three moves or five, or any *odd* number of moves, but never in an even number such as two or four no matter how much he doubles about. This can occasionally be a nuisance. Look at the next diagram.

Here White only awaits a chance to move his king out of the corner and queen his pawn, when he would easily win. At the moment he can not, for the black king is guarding his only two squares of exit. Suppose it were Black's turn to move, however; he could not move on to the black square below him because he could there be captured by the knight, so must move away from the white king allowing the latter to move as he wishes.

Diagram 52

Now suppose, on the other hand that it were White's turn to move. All he wants is to create the same position but with Black's turn to move, for that as we have seen is disastrous for Black. Can he do this? Never! Simply because the knight cannot move to 'save' or 'lose' a move, the black king can safely oscillate between the white square he is on and the black square below him, keeping the white king imprisoned, and nothing the knight can do will prevent him. The knight could roam away over the board but would always come back at just the wrong moment.

The 'Exchange'

Thus we have seen that both the knight and the bishop have weaknesses which make them, as a rule, worth less than a rook. If you win a rook in exchange for a bishop or knight, you are said to 'win the exchange' and you emerge from the transaction 'the exchange up'. Our word is less logical than most Continental languages, which term the operation 'winning the quality'.

Since the bishop and knight are inferior to the rook, they are often referred to as minor pieces, the rook and queen being 'major' or 'heavy' pieces.

Diagram 53

Occasionally a series of checks from your opponent's knight becomes irritating. Here is a tip which will enable you to escape the beast's unwelcome attention. He has a 'blind spot' two squares away from him diagonally, which he cannot attack in fewer than three moves. Move your king to this spot ('X' on the diagram) and the knight will not trouble you for a while.

A Bishop and Knight are practically equal in Value

Possibly the bishop's superior mobility very slightly more than compensates for his ineffectiveness on squares not of his colour; but there's little in it. Much depends on whether the bishop retains his partner; working together your bishops are strong, for whatever point one cannot attack, the other can. It is when one of them is exchanged off that the other's weakness becomes manifest. For this reason it is a definite advantage to have two bishops against your opponent's bishop and knight, other things being equal (at the same time, possibly too slight an advantage to produce a win out of an otherwise absolutely level position). To have two bishops against two knights is even better, probably sufficient for a win in the majority of positions; the bishops can utilise their superior mobility, whilst each commands the squares the other cannot.

The 'Two Bishops'

All this explains another common reference in the conversation and literature of chess enthusiasts. To say that one player has the *advantage of the two bishops* or simply that he has *the two bishops* implies that he has retained both bishops with which he started the game, but has managed to exchange off one or both of his opponent's.

When we come to endings where one player has lost every man but his king, and the other has only the king and a couple of minor pieces left, we find bishops superior to knights. King and two bishops can mate a king fairly easily (see Diagram 35 for the final position); king, bishop and knight can force a mate, but only with difficulty, the final position being as shown in the next diagram:

Diagram 54
King and two knights cannot

give mate at all unless the defender commits chess suicide.

It is rare that all the pawns are exchanged off whilst any pieces remain; much more commonly, the whole fight in the concluding stages of a tough game revolves round the efforts of the respective players to promote one or more of their few last pawns with the aid of the one or two pieces remaining uncaptured on each side. In this type of ending, a bishop is superior to a knight *if* the pawns are scattered about the board so that things are liable to happen in several different parts of the board. Thus the position in Diagram 55, which occurred in a game between two fairly evenly matched masters (Stoltz and Kashdan), though it looks even, was won by Black without great difficulty, making use of his bishop's longer stride.

Diagram 55

On the other hand, if the opposing groups of pawns are in

one compact mass, there is little between knight and bishop, and the former may even be superior.

In an average position, a rook is worth more than a knight and a pawn but less than a knight and two pawns. Substitute 'bishop' for 'knight' and you can say the same.

A bishop and knight are equal to a rook and two pawns; they are certainly better than a rook and one pawn. *With these types of balance of material, it is well to note that the value of the rook and pawn(s) tends to increase a little as the game goes on.* As we have seen, two bishops are slightly superior to, and two knights usually slightly inferior to, a bishop and a knight.

Open Files

A rook is at his best when stationed on an open file, an 'open' file being one on which stands no pawn of his own colour and no well-protected enemy pawn, either of which would cramp his effect. On the square he occupies at the commencement of the game, he is obviously badly hampered by the pawn in front of him.

Naturally the rook is 'safest' on the first rank of an open file; i.e. the rank from which all the pieces start. He should be held there, as a rule, until he can go through to the *seventh* rank,

which is the most powerful he can occupy, since it the one from which the enemy pawns start out and on which there will nearly always remain a few for him to attack:

Diagram 56

If either of the pawns which the rook is here threatening to capture moves forward to escape the attack, it merely exposes another pawn now sheltering behind it. Another reason why the rook is well stationed on the seventh rank is that it often traps the adverse king on the rank beyond, thus denying it access to seven-eighths of the board, just as the black king in Diagram 36 is shut off from the use of all but a few squares as a result of the position of White's queen.

Two rooks side by side on the seventh rank ('doubled' there) can exert a murderous effect.

Naturally, in special circumstances, a rook may be all-powerful on the fifth, sixth or any other rank; but the power it can generate on the seventh has to be experienced to be believed.

Whether a file is 'open' or not depends entirely on the presence or absence of *pawns* on it. It does not matter how many *pieces* there are on that file; it is still considered 'open' if clear of pawns. This is because pieces are so much more mobile than pawns and consequently less likely to remain on the file for any length of time. Pieces 'stay put' so seldom, in fact, that a queen or king on the same file as a hostile rook is in some danger, even though there may be two, or even three, pieces belonging to one side or the other on intervening squares. It is often advisable to anticipate the danger to a king or queen so placed, by moving it off the file.

Diagram 57

Unable to make use of any open file, a rook can become somewhat helpless. For instance, White cannot possibly win from

Diagram 57.

If there is only one open file it may pay you to 'double' your rooks on it, i.e. place one behind the other. They then reinforce each other's action; an enemy piece staying on the file can be captured by the first rook which, if recaptured, can then be avenged by his mate coming along from behind.

A Queen is roughly worth Two Rooks, or Three Minor Pieces

The queen is at her strongest in the middle of the game, the 'middlegame', after the situation has been partially simplified by the exchange of two or three pawns, and two or three pieces on each side. She can do little in the early stages, as she is too valuable to be risked out in the hurly-burly where a minor piece or pawn may snap her up. Towards the very end of a long and dourly-fought game, when only perhaps five or six men remain on the board, she may begin to lose her grip again. She then may be seriously troubled by, say, a rook or a bishop; with all her power, she remains only one piece and can only be in one place at a time. If one of her pawns can be simultaneously attacked by the two hostile pieces, as in Diagram 58, she may be unable to save it, as they can capture twice and she can only capture once.

Diagram 58

The most important factor in this kind of ending is the situation of the king opposed to her. If it is exposed, then she can acquire, to all intents, the ability to be in several places at once, by judiciously checking him. The opposing player has to attend to a check, usually by moving his king, and the position may remain essentially unchanged whilst the queen moves off in another direction, having virtually seized the opportunity to make two moves instead of one. If the adverse king is safely tucked away in a corner so that she cannot easily check him, she may be relatively ineffective, and the only chances of even making a fight may lie in sacrificing two or more pawns so as to break up the defences round him and expose him to her attentions.

If every other man except the kings has been exchanged off, a queen cannot normally win against a rook and a bishop or a rook and a knight, or even two bishops; whilst against a single rook or against two knights, she may have quite a difficult task. The addition of a single pawn on each side transforms endings of this type, because it adds a totally new aim (its promotion) to go for, and this complication of the issues diminishes to a marked extent the probability that the game will be drawn.

Two rooks combining well together in an endgame are usually a little too good for a queen.

All we have said about the drawbacks to the queen's power has to be taken with a grain of salt. Throughout all eventualities she remains a tremendously powerful piece which should be carefully guarded against incidental dangers, but at the same time employed to the fullest possible extent. Her effect on the game is so great that the whole nature of the combat alters when the queens are exchanged off; the 'middlegame' is said to end and the 'endgame' to begin.

If the other pieces are exchanged off before the queens, the character of the game changes much less abruptly as they go, the transition to the 'endgame' being more gradual and hazy but it can be said to come about when the last piece but one accompanying either queen disappears.

The King in the Endgame

Mention of the transition from middlegame to endgame brings us to consideration of the king, for it is precisely when the endgame begins that he ceases to be a helpless passenger and becomes a useful member of the community. In the beginning he is a liability. Danger to him is danger to the whole cause, so that it is folly to parade him in the open when seven hostile pieces are prowling about the board, eager for his blood. Risk him out in the open and he may be mated in two or three catastrophic moves. It may even pay your opponent to sacrifice a queen or more to draw your king into the open. As a rule, he is best tucked away in safety by 'castling'. The safer way, nine times out of ten, is with the nearer rook. This, in the main, for three reasons:

(a) Castling this side can normally come earlier, since there are only two intervening pieces to be cleared away, instead of three;

(b) After castling, the king protects all the pawns in front of him, whereas, castling with the other rook, the pawn on the edge of the board is left unprotected and might allow an entry to hostile pieces; and

(c) In castling with the further rook, he moves over to the same side of the board as the hostile queen.

Turn back to pages 24-25 (Diagrams 24-27), where positions before and after castling are given, and verify these statements.

As soon as the endgame is reached, the king emerges from retirement and begins to pay a positive part in the struggle. This is the real definition of the endgame: the part of the game in which the king can play an effective part. It is one of the hallmarks of a good player to be able to recognise almost instinctively when the endgame has been reached. In many games, there comes a stage at which the only correct plan is to bring the king out and advance him as far in the centre as possible; when to overlook this fact for as much as one move, and start his advance one single move too late, may jeopardise your chances.

You see, the king may be a plodder, moving one step at a time from beginning to end (his two-square jump when castling is only a scurry for safety), but he has his points. He can move along 'any' of the eight different directions of the simple compass, being the only piece beside the queen which can do so; this means that, by choosing the appropriate method of approach, he can go right up to a rook or a bishop or a knight or a pawn and capture it if allowed; even the mighty rook is vulnerable along a diagonal. He can move backwards, and tack about, which makes him the superior of a pawn. He can wander all round the board and make a real nuisance of himself. It only requires that there should not be enough hostile pieces left to create real danger of mate to him.

On a strictly statistical count of the number of squares 'under his eye', such as we employed in comparing rooks with bishops and knights, he comes out as stronger than a knight, for at best he controls eight squares, the same as a knight, and at worst he never controls fewer than three. This is an exaggeration of his real strength, even in an endgame, because of his sensitivity to attack.

So far, I have given you a lot of facts, but very little advice. If you only read between the lines, however, you will find this chapter full of advice. There is a lesson in almost every remark.

For instance, I mentioned that a rook is worth roughly a bishop-and-a-half. In other words, if you perceive a chance of capturing one of your opponent's rooks for one of your bishops, seize it! I showed that two bishops are worth rather more than twice as much as one bishop. In other words, you must try to preserve your two bishops or, if one has to be exchanged off, see that you exchange it off for one of your opponent's bishops or obtain some compensation otherwise. I

showed that a pawn gains in value as it advances towards promotion - hence, if you think that one of your pawns has a good chance of getting right through to the queening square, push it forward as hard as you can. I showed that a knight is more useful than a bishop in a blocked position. Consequently, if you feel that the position is becoming blocked, try to keep your knights on the board rather than your bishops and, by the same token, if your opponent has obtained the advantage of the two bishops, do all you can to keep the position blocked so that their mobility has little scope. If, in the closing stages, your opponent's only remaining piece is a bishop and yours is a knight, try to exchange off all the pawns except those in one part of the board. If you are materially in arrears and fighting against the probability of defeat, try to exchange off the last few pawns, leaving pieces only. Whenever an exchange of pieces occurs, ask yourself 'Is it time to bring my king out yet?' And so on, and so on.

Protection

I have more than once lightly touched on the principle of 'protection' of one man by another. 'Guarding' is just the same thing, so is 'defending'. In the narrow sense of the word to 'attack' a man means to simply threaten to take it. There are so many men on the board (they occupy half the squares to start with) that it is silly to try to avoid all attacks from hostile pieces by moving your attacked men away. More - it would be a sheer impossibility.

The sensible and universal course is to arrange your men so that any liable to be captured are insured against disaster by the fact that the hostile man capturing could immediately be itself recaptured. That is to say, you 'protect' them. For instance, the next diagram shows a rook, a knight and a bishop each protected by a pawn.

Diagram 59

Any hostile piece capturing yours could be immediately recapture by the pawn. It would not pay your opponent to capture your knight with any piece of greater value than a knight, because by recapturing you would get the better of the bargain. If your piece is captured by one of equal value, still no harm may be done; a black knight and a white knight disappear together from the board and the *status quo* is practically unchanged. Your pawn will have been moved forward a rank diagonally, that is all.

Any man except the king may be protected in this way, by the counter-threat to capture; and any man whatever can supply the protection. In one and the same game, you may see kings protecting pawns, rooks protecting rooks, queens protecting knights, knights protecting pawns, bishops protecting rooks, etc., etc. It is rare that a queen is protected, in fact only when she is attacked by the enemy queen, for any other hostile piece would gladly take her and suffer recapture. When attacked, she must usually flee. Pawns, on the other hand, have to be continuously protected or kept where the danger of their being attacked is small. Moreover, it is rarely good to allocate to a piece the menial task of defending a pawn, so that you should normally plan the positioning of your whole body of pawns as one scheme, as many of them mutually protected, or safe from attack, as possible.

The normal line of pawns protecting each other is, of course, diagonal. An extreme case is that of the black pawns in Diagram 48, where every black pawn protects the one in front of it and the only one out of the six that a white piece could contemplate capturing, in normal circumstances, is the hindmost of all.

Your king cannot be captured at all under the rules, so it is pointless to prepare to recapture a piece that captures him. He is customarily protected in a different way, by screening him from hostile action by two or three pawns and pieces. As we saw in Diagrams 39-41, we must not let the men who are thus sheltering him interfere unduly with his own mobility, or the result may be disastrous.

A piece once attacked and once protected may be attacked by a second enemy piece. It must then be either moved or provided with an additional protector, otherwise after recapture of a capturer by the defending piece, there will come a capture by the second attacker and two men will have been lost in exchange for one. Another and another attacker, and another and another defender, may be brought to bear on one square under dispute and finally quite a massacre take place there. One player captures on that square; then the other recaptures; the first captures with yet another piece; his opponent captures with a second of his pieces, and so on. It is simplest when calculating whether or not a certain square is safe for occupation, not to try to imagine all these captures taking

place, but to count how many friendly men, and how many hostile men, bear on that square. If there are three men attacking a knight, but only two defending it, it could be captured in the certainty that, when the captures and recaptures are all over, some man of the original capturer's side will remain in possession and the owner of the knight will have lost a man in the skirmish. Diagram 60 shows such a case - a pretty complicated one, where the white knight is four times defended but five times attacked. If it is White's turn to move, he must either give it additional protection, or move it away. If it is Black's turn, by capturing it he can assure himself of winning a piece.

Diagram 60

When reckoning out a train of possible captures like this, we must never omit to take into account the *quality* of the various men involved. The knight or the bishop in Diagram 59 might be attacked by three enemy pieces at a time but if these three enemy pieces are the queen and the two rooks, it would not pay Black to make the capture, owing to their greater value. Consequently, there would be no need to provide the knight with extra protection.

The Figures are only Foundations

The little table we gave on page 34 provides the foundations for any calculation on these lines. Whenever contemplating a possible exchange of pieces other than an elementary knight-for-knight or queen-for-queen, you can mentally refer back to this table. Suppose Black had two rooks bearing on to the knight in Diagram 59. By capturing with one rook and then capturing with the other, the pawn which recaptures the first rook, Black would obtain a knight and a pawn in exchange for a rook. Is it worth it? No, because a rook is worth more than a knight and a pawn, so that Black would lose by the transaction.

Note that I only say 'foundations'! It may quite often pay you to give up a rook for a knight and pawn (if, for instance, the rook is badly placed and both the knight and the pawn well-placed). *Never overlook positional considerations*, or the table on page 34 will hamper you as much as help.

4 First Chess Games

Touch and Move

It is well to cultivate, in the very beginning of your chess career, a clean-cut style of play. Do not get into the habit of hovering over the pieces with your hand whilst considering what move to make or, still worse, picking up a piece, placing it on a square and then looking round in all directions to see if it is safe there before letting it go. This last method has a germ of utility in your first few games for, until you become familiar with the moves of the various men, you will often inadvertently put yours where they can be captured, so that your first care must be to avoid mistakes like this; in fact, you have to build up a reserve of instinctive caution. But you should train yourself to 'imagine' your man moved onto the square you intend. Make up your mind whether it is safe there or not, and whether that is the best move you can make or not, before you touch it at all. In all chess but the most casual kind the 'touch and move' rule is insisted on: if you touch one of your own men, you must move it; if you touch one of your opponent's men, you must take it if legally possible. If you touch more than one of your own men, your opponent can decide which one you must move. Above all, if you find you have blundered, after making a move, it is most unsporting to take back that move and make another instead. To allow yourself the luxury of fingering the pieces vaguely when playing some intimate friend is to sow the seeds of many an unexpected loss on technicalities when, later on, you meet a stranger in a serious game. You may develop a rooted habit which condemns you to weeks of annoyance and maybe unpleasantness.

It sometimes happens that you come up against somebody who does not stick to 'touch and move', but repeatedly snatches back a piece just as you are going to take advantage of some blunder. What are you to do? Here is my studied advice. If the game is a casual one, say nothing but continue to adhere rigidly to the rule yourself. Your opponent is only handicapping himself by his self-indulgence and before very long you will find the stricter training you are giving yourself beginning to pay its dividends in the form of won games. If, on the other hand, it is a match or tournament game or any contest of a serious nature, you should pluck up your courage and insist, gently but quite firmly, on observance of the rules. After all, if your opponent were to move a bishop like a knight, you would feel perfectly justified in protesting. (They say Napoleon, a keen chess-player, used to resort to this silly trick when getting the worst of it!) Why, then, feel diffident in applying another rule which, among the laws of chess, is given just as important a place as that regulating the moves of the various pieces? If you are going to play chess, then play according to the rules, all of which are equally binding.

This does not mean that you must sit throughout with your hands in your pockets, in mortal terror lest you accidentally brush a piece or pawn with your finger or cuff. Not even the most deadly-keen chess-master would try to penalise you for a mere mishap. Again a carelessly-executed move or a jar to the table might leave a man placed on the edge of a square instead of the middle. Is it to remain there for the rest of the game, disturbing the calculations of both contestants, because each fears to adjust

it lest he be called upon to move or take it? Obviously this would be absurd. Under such circumstances as this the murmured pass-word *j'adoube* (pronounced 'jadoob' and meaning 'I adjust') gives you the right to correct the positions of as many men as you please. Say this clearly and you can make any adjustment.

Though you will win and lose many games in your early chess experience through you or your opponent leaving odd men to be captured for nothing, you should never assume that chess consists of little more than a 'picking up of unconsidered trifles'. Edgar Allan Poe made this mistake in thinking chess less subtle than draughts. Very soon you should start to evolve plans and the first time one of these, however crude, succeeds, you will gain a glimpse of the rapturous attraction that the game has in store for you.

The Time-Control

Once upon a time, any player could take as long as he liked over any move. Whoever got the worse of the earlier stages of a game might, by deliberately spending inordinate amounts of time over every subsequent move, recover lost ground by subjecting his opponent to sheer boredom and weariness. It is a wonder, and an everlasting tribute to its intrinsic charm, that chess ever survived.

About a century ago, the idea of controlling the time allowance for each player was adopted, first sand-glasses then special clocks coming into use. These revolutionised the game.

A modern chess clock really consists of two clocks, each of which works independently of the other. Each records the time consumed by one of the two players. When you have made your move, you press down the knob on the top of the clock on the side nearest to you. This automatically raises the other side, stops your own clock and starts your opponent's. As long as he is engaged in thinking out his reply move, his clock goes on whilst yours remains stationary. As soon as he makes his move, he presses down his knob, stopping his own clock and re-starting yours which continues to tick whilst you in turn cogitate on your reply.

The time registered on either of the clocks at any moment thus represents the total time expended by the player whose time it is measuring, over all the moves he has made up to then. If you take a minute over your first move, two minutes over your second and nine minutes over your third then your clock, as you press the knob on making your third move, should stand at twelve minutes (one plus two plus nine) past the hour. Naturally the minute-hand is the one

you watch, and it matters little where the hour hands stand at the commencement of a game as long as the minute-hands are correctly adjusted at the appropriate zero mark.

There may be a see-sawing bar instead of two knobs.

The 'Flag'

Each clock has a little red 'flag' suspended near the twelve o'clock mark, which is slowly raised to a horizontal position by the minute hand as the latter approaches that mark, and falls again the moment it passes. A fairly common time schedule is twenty moves per hour, which means that each player is allowed an hour for each twenty moves he makes. In the majority of cases, both players make their twenty moves well within the allotted hour but it occasionally happens, when the game has been unusually difficult or complicated, that one or both have difficulty in doing so. If a player fails to make his twentieth move before his flag drops for the first time, he automatically forfeits the game, even though he may have an overwhelmingly superior position and may complete his quota of moves an instant later. Each player must likewise have made forty moves before his flag falls again at the end of a further hour of his time, and so on.

Rarely are more than 24 moves to the hour called for. On the other hand, tournament and match games are usually played to a slower schedule, say 18 or 20 moves to the hour; or even forty moves to two-and-a-half hours, which is in some ways an improvement since it minimises the interference of time with the game - you can forget about your clock for four hours or more, by when the game may be over.

You can, of course, space out your time-allowance as you please. The opening moves of familiar openings are usually played quickly by both sides so that they can utilise the time gained for a good long 'think' when the position becomes involved. If there is no time control until the end of the second hour, a player may take three-quarters of an hour, or even an hour, over a single move. This would have sown the seeds of boredom in the old days, but it can never annoy anybody now. If you have to wait three-quarters of an hour for a move, you know that you will never have to wait so long again in that game, also that your opponent has saddled himself with the task of making many more moves in a very short time.

You Can Get Up!

There is not the least need for you to remain in your seat for this period. In fact, it is not a procedure to be recommended; staring fixedly at the same object for three or four hours is enough to hypnotise anybody into stupidity. Leading masters walk away after almost every move; etiquette only demands that you should rise from and return to your seat quietly so as not to disturb your opponent. The average tournament or match room is thronged by players wandering from board to board, having a glance at the positions reached in other games whilst their opponent is busy on their own. In the train on the way back from a match you may discover that practically every member of the team knows something about what has happened on the other boards. Whilst walking about the room you can exchange many a jest, go and have a drink, strike up a new acquaintance; chess is not anti-social. Naturally, you keep an eye on your game throughout these wanderings and it is an understood convention that when your opponent moves, you may break off any conversation at a moment's notice without offence, to return to your game.

You might ask 'How am I to know when I have made 20 moves?' This question is answered in our chapter on 'notation'; you are supposed to keep a score of the game as you go along. I have explained the modern system of time control at this

stage to correct the popular mis-
conception unfortunately quite
widespread, that chess-players
frequently go off to sleep or grow
beards whilst their opponents are
considering a single move. The
situation is vastly otherwise. In
many games you will long for
more time than you are allowed,
to unravel all the perplexing
complexities; you may be battling
against shortage of time from the
first move to the last. This may
be nerve wracking and certainly
makes the game exciting. As I
once mentioned in a broadcast, I
have dangled from a mountain
crag with a 500-feet drop below
me, and found it a pretty tense
experience; but no tenser than
many a gruelling game of chess,
where every decision had to be
made against time.

Chess clocks are not essential;
millions of friendly games are
played without them. Should you
ever find yourself becoming
bored by an opponent's slowness,
however, you will find comfort in
the knowledge that in serious
chess they are almost universal.

Speed Chess

The clock has made chess a game
for the young. The time-
allowances are generous enough
not to discount patience and te-
nacity but sufficiently stringent to
reward enterprise.

The speeding-up of chess has
not stopped at this routine clock
control but has passed on to various forms of quick chess. One
form of this is 'lightning chess',
in which only a few seconds are
allowed per move, with instant
disqualification for any player a
fraction of a second too late with
any move. A buzzer sounds for
one second, at regular intervals
five or ten seconds apart; and
during the second it is sounding
the player whose turn it is to
move must pick up his piece,
move it to the chosen square and
move his finger from it. He has
the intervening five or ten seconds to consider and decide on
his move. Naturally lightning
chess has nothing like the stand-
ing of the normal game but one or
two sessions are held during
some chess congresses in which
quite famous players may partici-
pate with gusto. The light-
heartedness of players and specta-
tors alike at these sessions is an
eye-opener to non-chess-players.
Naturally the play is far from correct, good players in their haste
making elementary blunders
which arouse uncontrollable gusts
of laughter.

No chess club should omit
lightning chess from its annual
programme, for it can be a tumul-
tuously successful diversion. If it
is not practicable to obtain or
make one of the special buzzing
clocks required, one self-
sacrificing member can equip
himself with a cheap electric

buzzer and watch with a seconds hand and provide the noises-off. Or he can even bang a tin can. Another member should act as umpire, disqualifying without mercy all players who overstep their time-allowance.

There is another, even more popular, type of quick chess: 'five-minute chess' in which each player is allotted just five minutes on his clock.

The moves are *not* counted.

The game may be won or lost in the ordinary way of play before either player exceeds his time; but if not, the first whose flag falls has lost.

The drawback to 'five-minute chess' is that if both players run short of time, a wild scramble may develop. With each in turn trying to make a move and press his clock knob in a fraction of a second, I have more than once seen the clock knocked off the table or otherwise damaged.

The great advantage of five-minute chess is that time can often be saved over simple positions (for instance the first few moves of the game can be played in a flash) which can then be devoted to more complex situations which merit deeper attention. It produces a game of higher quality than 'buzzer' chess.

Naturally the clocks can be set to ten or any other number of minutes if preferred, but five is more popular. A stronger player may be handicapped by being allowed only, say, four minutes to his opponent's five.

Both forms of lightning chess have advanced considerably in popularity in recent years. Once they were just 'fun'. Now national championships are fought out.

In New York, lightning chess is known as 'rapid transit'; in Buenos Aires, as 'ping-pong'.

Nowadays rapid chess events, in which players play five or six games in a single day, with a time-limit of 30 or 40 minutes each for the whole game, are extremely popular at weekends up and down the country.

Unfinished Games

If a game has to be broken off for resumption later, the last participant before the adjournment does not disclose his move to his opponent - or even make it on the board - but writes it on a piece of paper, seals it up in an envelope and hands it to an independent person for safe keeping. This is called 'sealing a move'. In the Middle Ages, travelling chess players used to accompany fairs and engage in matches against local 'cracks'; unfinished games were adjourned and moves sealed in the presence of lawyers specifically summoned to attest the positions and take charge of the sealed moves.

Nowadays, when clocks are

used, a note of the time taken accompanies the move. The system ensures, in a simple way, that no player gets the chance to seek assistance, or to move the pieces about in private, at any stage whilst 'deciding his next move'.

In weekend tournaments the most popular form of concluding a game that has gone beyond the time-control is the quickplay finish, in which each player is allocated a further 15 or 20 minutes to complete the game.

5 Elements of Combination

The 'Fork'

Early in your career as a chess player you may lose games with annoying frequency through allowing a 'fork'. See the diagrammed position. Here the knight can capture the pawn, giving check to the king which has to move, and then capturing the rook. Naturally, this is supposed to represent only a part of the whole position, there being other pieces and pawns not shown.

and a rook for nothing. Even if Black manages to capture the knight later on (and it is true that the latter sometimes finds it a little difficult to make his way out of the corner again), he finishes with only a knight for a rook and a pawn, which is a very bad bargain.

This position is very easily reached from the position of the men at the commencement of the game. Set them up as in Diagram 23 and observe that, after two moves by each player, the following position is possible:

Diagram 61

Diagram 62

A move like this can win the game, since White gains a pawn

It is not difficult to see that White's two moves were made

with his knight and Black's with a pawn and his queen. White is *already* in a position to win Black's rook by a move exactly like that shown above. Once you are really familiar with the knight's move you will never be caught napping by this trick; but in a more involved form it occurs in many a master game and it illustrates a theme of the greatest importance, called a 'divergent attack' or 'fork'. The knight after it has captured the pawn attacks king and rook simultaneously; it is said to 'fork' them.

Here is another example of the knight's fork, where it involves a rook and a queen, instead of a rook and a king. The effect is again great; the queen must move or she would be captured; then the rook may be captured.

Diagram 63

The knight's fork has a certain insidiousness which other men's forks lack, partly because the knight is not a very valuable

piece in itself; but any and every piece can 'fork', i.e. simultaneously attack two hostile pieces at once. So can a pawn. Here is an example of a pawn forking a rook and a knight:

Diagram 64

One of the attacked pieces can move away; the other must be abandoned for capture. In the next diagram too, the right-hand pawn can 'fork' the bishop and queen by advancing one square.

Diagram 65

Although either the bishop or the queen could then capture him, his fellow-pawn, who is correctly placed to protect him, could then recapture so that at worst White will gain a bishop in return for two pawns.

A bishop can also 'fork'. For instance, here a bishop is forking two rooks (Diagram 66):

Diagram 66

Diagram 67 shows another kind of bishop 'fork':

Diagram 67

The rook in the next diagram is forking a knight and a bishop. Owing to the high value of the rook, its 'fork' has not quite the same terror in many cases (the converse effect to the knight whose fork is deadly because of the knight's low value). White would be ill-advised to capture a bishop or knight with a rook if his opponent could recapture. So that here, for instance, if either the bishop or the knight were already protected, Black would only need to attend to the threat to the other. Whereas in Diagram 63, it would not matter a jot if the queen or the rook were protected, for the knight would gladly give itself up in exchange for either.

Diagram 68

The queen's fork is troublesome, in spite of her great value, because it can be set up easily as a result of her mobility. The queen can fork along a rank or file, as in the case of the rook fork; along two diagonals, as in the case of the bishop (a queen instead of the bishop in Diagrams 66 and 67, or instead of the rook in Diagram 68, would attack the two forked pieces just the same); or along a rank or file and a diagonal. Diagram 69 illustrates the first of these, Diagram 70 the second and Diagrams 71 and 72 the third. The third kind is the most deadly and the one for which you must most carefully watch; it is the kind that neither the bishop nor the rook can set up, for it makes use of both their powers. Don't forget that the queen may fork like a rook as in Diagram 69; or like a bishop as in Diagram 70.

Diagram 70

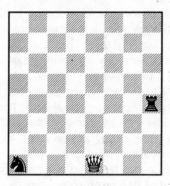

Diagram 71

Diagram 69

The threat of attacks like this from a queen is so great that you should take care to ensure that as many of your men as possible (and the important ones for certain) are protected whenever your opponent's queen has freedom.

Diagram 72

In none of Diagrams 63 to 72 has an attacked man been the king. Substitute the king for any of the attacked pieces, and the fork gains in power for there is now no question which of the attacked pieces is to move, or which it is advisable to protect. The king must be seen to, the other attacked man being left in the lurch. This is one of the many reasons why the king should not be brought out into the middle of the board at an early stage in the game; he might be subjected to some check form which he could easily escape on his own account, but through the checking piece simultaneously attacking another man, that man may be lost.

Whilst the effect of a fork is greater the more valuable the men attacked and the less valuable the man 'forking', any sort of fork whatever can influence and even decide the result of a game. The fork of two unprotected pawns by a queen, by leading to the loss of one of them, might decide a game between masters.

The king, as the most sensitive of all the men and the one who dare not come out into the open until some of the other pieces have been exchanged off, is rarely able to 'fork' two hostile pieces, but when he is, the very rarity and unexpectedness of the happening may produce a tremendous effect. For instance, a world championship game was once won in this way, the posi-

tion in Diagram 73 being reached.

Diagram 73

Here the white king, is forking the black rook and knight, one of which must perish.

As the one piece certain of survival into the endgame, the king often gets an opportunity to fork two *pawns* or a pawn and a piece, as shown in the next two diagrams.

Diagram 74

Diagram 75

Playing against weak or inex-
perienced opponents, you will
often have an opportunity to stage
a decisive fork. Against a
stronger opponent, you have to
'manufacture' your own opportunities - you will rarely be presented with them. Here is a typical example of manufacturing
your own opportunity:

Diagram 76

Each side has exactly the same
number and quality of pieces and

pawns. White has a spectacular
move at his disposal. He captures
the knight with his queen, giving
check to the black king and also
threatening the black queen. This
is a fork of the black king and
queen by the white queen. On the
surface it looks like sheer mad-
ness, for the white queen is unprotected and can be captured by
the black; this is naturally a perfectly good way for Black to get
out of his check (by 'capture of
the checking piece') and, in fact,
the best. So Black takes the white
queen. Now comes the real 'fork'
which White manufactured for
himself. Can you see it? Set out
the pieces, as in Diagram 76, on a
board and play first 'queen takes
knight, check' for White and then
'queen takes queen' for Black in
reply. Do you see that now White
has manoeuvred the black queen
into such a position that he can
'fork' Black's king and queen
with his knight? The resulting
position, is as in Diagram 77.

Diagram 77

Both the black king and the black queen are attacked; the king must move out of check and then the queen is captured. White gave up his queen for one little knight to start with, but has now regained it for nothing; so that, by the whole transaction, he has gained a knight. It is interesting to note that, in Diagram 77, if the white knight were not to capture the queen, the queen could mate White next move by playing down to the first rank, the mating position being of the same type as that shown in Diagram 32. How exactly the whole thing had to be calculated! To win a piece, White risked the loss of his queen, and being mated - or perhaps that is putting it too strongly, for he would not have dared to sacrifice his queen had he not calculated that he must recover her next move.

by means of a fork cleverly brought about (Diagram 78). Black appears to have the better of it, for he has an extra pawn. But White plays 'rook takes pawn'. If Black recaptures with the pawn which was protecting the one captured, the resulting position is as shown in Diagram 78. Now White takes the recapturing pawn with his bishop, at the same time 'forking' both black rooks, one of which he picks up for nothing next move. White gives up a rook but obtains in return two pawns and a rook, so that he is two pawns up as a result of the skirmish and has turned an apparently lost game into a probable win. Black would, in fact, do better not to recapture on his first move at all.

Diagram 79

Diagram 78

Here is another position which offers a typical chance of winning

All in all, the 'fork' is by far the most powerful thematic weapon in chess.

The 'Skewer'

That great chess teacher, Edgar Pennell, invented a perfect kitchen analogy to the 'fork' when he applied the term 'skewer' to the sort of thing that can arise from the next diagram. Here the white rook can capture the pawn, giving check to the king which must move and let the rook through to capture the queen beyond. Just as a fork is something with more than one prong which can stick into two lumps of meat on your plate at the same time, so the skewer is something that pushes right through a lump of meat and out the other side.

Diagram 80

Skewers are encountered more rarely than forks, as they require a bigger free area on the board for their operation and cannot be set up by knights, pawns or kings. Moreover, for a skewer to be effective, the middle man has to be of a value greater than the skewering man, which is seldom the case as the cheapest man which can set up a skewer is the bishop. Here is a form of bishop skewer which is occasionally encountered:

Diagram 81

It is little use moving the attacked rook, because there is another behind.

The next class of manoeuvre we shall examine is of paramount importance. It is an inverted skewer, in which the intermediate man is not worth as much as the one behind.

The 'Pin'

When a man is deterred from moving by the fact that, in doing so, he would open up a line for an enemy piece to capture a valuable man of his own side, he is said to be 'pinned' or to be suffering from a 'pin'. An example or two will make this clearer than any amount of explanation. Here, for instance, is an example of the earliest pin which can occur in an actual game. Each side has made one pawn move and one piece move, and now the knight which Black has moved out from its original square is 'pinned' by a white bishop against Black's queen. If the knight were to move now, it would open the way for the white bishop to capture the black queen, which would be disastrous for Black.

Diagram 82

Consequently the knight is under restraint, in fact, in ninety-nine cases out of a hundred, it is immobilised; the one exceptional case where it will be free to move is when it has the opportunity to do some brilliant piece of work which justifies giving up the queen. Now look at another position which can likewise arise after two moves on each side:

Diagram 83

Here it is a white knight which is pinned by a black bishop and now it is the white king which will be captured if the knight moves. But the king cannot be captured! Quite true; this is a somewhat nastier type of pin than the first, for whereas, in Diagram 82, the knight could move in the exceptional case where it had brilliant work to do, this knight is prevented by the rules of the game from moving in any circumstances whatever. You are not allowed to put your own king into check: that is what White would be doing if he were to move the knight.

There is no 'fatal' danger in the two pins we have illustrated; they can be easily neutralised, for instance, by attacking the bishop by pawns so as to drive it off the threatening diagonal or (better as a rule) by moving a minor piece, such as a bishop, in between the pinned piece and the king or queen against which it is pinned. The danger is partly psychological. You become so accustomed to regarding a piece as being able to move in such-and-such a way that you are liable to overlook the fact that, when pinned, it cannot move at all. Thus you (playing White) may think that your bishop in Diagram 84, is protected by your knight. Your opponent takes the bishop with his queen and you realise to your horror that you cannot recapture - your knight is as useless as a lump of wood - it *cannot* move.

Diagram 84

It cannot move! That is the second weakness of the pinned piece. 'He who fights and runs away may live to fight another day,' but a pinned piece cannot run away and often succumbs, as a consequence, to some attack which would otherwise be quite harmless. Here is a position (Diagram 85) in which the black knight is pinned against the black

king by a white bishop.

Diagram 85

The knight cannot move. White can advance his pawn, attacking the knight, and that wretched piece, which could normally evade a pawn's attack with ease, succumbs without a fight.

Diagram 86

Diagram 86 shows another example of a pin. Black dare not move the pawn away from the attack or he would lose his queen.

All these have been pins by bishops; a type of pin which is most dangerous because of the bishop's small value, which often makes it profitable to exchange him for the man he pins. The rook's pin can be troublesome too, one of the most common types being shown in Diagram 87, where White has quickly moved out the knight and bishop near his king, and castled, whereas Black has neglected to move his king to safety but mistakenly grabbed a pawn in the middle of the board.

further attack it with one of his pawns next move and capture it with that pawn the move after. Black could protect it with his queen, by moving that piece in front of his king; this would not relieve the pin, since the knight, if it now moves, would expose the queen.

The next diagram shows pins by a queen along both her lines of force at one.

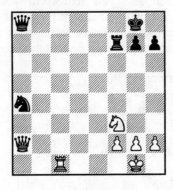

Diagram 88

Diagram 87

You may find it interesting to try to work out the six moves on each side by which this position was reached.

White can now win a piece in a couple of moves. He moves his free rook one square to the left, pinning the black knight against the black king, and threatening to capture it. Whichever way Black chooses to protect it, White can

The white queen is pinning the rook against the king, the knight against her opposite number.

You must avail yourself of pins and fight against them. Seize any chance you can of setting up a profitable pin; if you cannot win an enemy piece, you can thus render it temporarily useless, which is the next best thing.

If one of your own men is pinned, it is not always advisable to take hurried steps to relieve the pin; there may be other more important things to be done first.

Where there is danger that your pinned piece may soon be further attacked, e.g. by a pawn, immediate attention is required of course. Diagram 84 teaches us one incidental aspect of a pin which must never be overlooked. Suppose you are White, and Black has just played his bishop to its present post, pinning your knight. By this, he attacks your *bishop* more than your knight, for he deprives it of the protection the knight was offering it, by rendering the knight useless. If you overlook the fact that it is really the bishop which is attacked, you may come to grief. You may, for example, seek to relieve the pin by driving the black bishop away, by advancing your extreme left-hand pawn one square with the threat to capture it. This would lose a piece, because Black would capture your knight with his bishop, 'check!', destroying the protection to your own bishop. You would have to recapture the bishop with your pawn and Black would then capture your now unprotected bishop with his queen, gaining a piece in the skirmish.

As in the case of a 'fork', when up against a good player you will have to manufacture your own opportunities for pins. A typical chance arises in the position of Diagram 89, which rather resembles Diagram 87. Here Black's knight seems safe, being once attacked and once protected. White captures it, however, and

Black then realises that if he captures, his queen can be pinned against his king by the white rook's moving one square to the left; after which the most Black could ever obtain, in exchange for his queen, would be a rook. Note that White's rook must be supported when it goes to pin the queen, otherwise it could be captured by the very piece it is pinning and attacking.

Diagram 89

Diagram 90

Diagram 91

Diagram 92

To help familiarise you with pins, whether manufactured or just left available through weak moves by your opponent, diagrams 90-92 show three more pins by bishops, each of which prove disastrous for one player.

In Diagram 92 Black dare not move his knight because his rook would then be captured. In Diagram 91, Black's queen is pinned against his king and White is threatening to capture it for only

a bishop next move - one of the nastiest pins imaginable.

In Diagram 90, his rook is pinned against his queen. In each of the three cases White is about to win some pleasant prize and a point is, that *he should have been willing in each case to sacrifice anything less in the previous play, to bring this situation about.* For instance, in Diagram 90, where he is about to win a rook for nothing, he would have been perfectly justified in sacrificing a knight or a bishop and a pawn, to obtain this position; in Diagram 92, he is only going to win a knight, the weakest piece there is, but even for this purpose it might have paid him to give up one of his own knights, if his general *position* were improved by the whole skirmish.

We mentioned that a piece pinned against a queen can, exceptionally, move where it can do brilliant work which justifies giving away the queen.

Diagram 93

Diagram 93 depicts a situation which is an excellent example of this type.

This position can arise after four moves on each side (it is an interesting incidental exercise to work out what they might have been).

White's knight can take the pawn!

Now, if Black's bishop grabs White's queen, White's bishop can capture the pawn which is by Black's king, giving check.

The 'Half-Pin'

The half-pin only occurs rarely in play but is common in chess problems. Once you understand the pin, the half-pin explains itself. There are now *two* men between the valuable piece and the hostile piece on its line; for instance, in Diagram 103, the rook is half-pinning Black's knight and bishop against his king, the point being that if either should move off that line, the other would be pinned.

Diagram 94

Diagram 95

There is only one legal reply for Black: his king must come one square down the board - whereupon White's other knight moves in and mates him, the final position being as our next diagram.

After White's first move in Diagram 93, Black is not 'compelled' to take the queen but any alternative move leaves him at least one pawn down.

'Overburdened' Men

In each of the next three diagrams White, to move, can win a piece, because one of the black men is 'overburdened'.

In Diagram 96, White captures the bishop with his knight; if the black pawn recaptures, he can capture the rook with his king for nothing.

Diagram 96

Diagram 97

In Diagram 97, he captures the knight with the queen; if the black rook then recaptures the queen, White can move his rook through to the topmost rank, checkmating Black in a way similar to Diagram 32.

In Diagram 98, White would dearly like to move his bishop one square to the North-west. Black's queen would then be

pinned against her king, and ultimately lost in exchange for the bishop, like the queen in Diagram 91 - if only Black's knight were not so placed as to be ready to capture the bishop when it moves that one square North-west.

White captures the rook! If Black now recaptures with the knight, he permits White to set up that fatal pin after all, since the knight has been decoyed away and no longer covers the critical square.

Diagram 98

In each of the three diagrams, a black man had more duties than it could cope with. In Diagram 96, the pawn could not protect both the bishop and the rook. In Diagram 97, the black rook had to guard the knight and also prevent White from mating with his rook on the back rank. In Diagram 98, the black knight had to protect the rook and also to prevent the white bishop from pinning the queen.

It should be obvious enough, from these examples, what is meant by an 'overburdened' piece or pawn.

If one of your opponent's men has too much to do, try to exploit this. Conversely, don't overwork any of your own men; try to distribute the work among them. Overwork spells breakdown in chess as it does in real life!

6 Pawns

A great player once stated 'the pawns are the soul of chess'. In spite of their weakness, they are *important*. As we have already seen, they can do noble service in the protection of pieces. Their very weakness sometimes aids. If one of your knights is attacked by a queen, you can ignore the threat altogether if it is protected, since your opponent would be silly to capture the knight when you are ready to capture the queen in exchange. A knight attacked by a pawn, however, must move whether protected or not, or otherwise be lost in exchange for the pawn - a bad bargain!

You might, considering this, think it pleasant to chase your opponent's pieces about with your pawns. You could chivvy them from square to square; from every little thrust, they could seek refuge only in flight. This procedure soon becomes unprofitable for the attacker, because pawns can never return from any foray - a pawn can only move forward, never backward. Hence, if attacked itself, it lacks the great resource open to a piece - flight. If, to evade an attack, it *must*

move, it can only go forward, and every step takes it nearer to the enemy lines, its peril multiplying in an increasing ratio. In the vast majority of cases a pawn, when attacked, must stay where it is and seek protection; if that can be supplied by a fellow-pawn, little harm may be done but, if a piece has to be pressed into service for the job, that pawn is becoming a nuisance to its possessor. Pieces are too valuable to be wasted on the menial task of protecting a pawn - it is like a fishing vessel asking for special protection from a battleship.

To Have to Protect Pawns by Pieces is Bad

Now do you see the drawbacks of too much chivvying of your opponent's pieces with your pawns? Very soon your rather scrappy attack will peter out, as the pieces finally reach safety. Then you will suddenly find your pawns badly scattered about the board, some of them far afield. Your opponent will threaten first one, then another - this will be all the easier, because they are so near his lines. You cannot retreat them. You may manage to defend one or two by other pawns, but elsewhere pieces will have to shoulder the task; moreover, remember that a single pawn may be attacked by more than one enemy piece, so that two, three, or even more men have to go to his rescue. At best, you will manage to protect every threatened point but then all your pieces will be tied down to defence; not one will be free to move until your opponent permits. Your opponent will be able to call the tune and control the course of the game; he would have to be a bad player not to find some chance of converting this big initiative into a win; a typical method is to shift the attack suddenly form one side of the board to the other, using for this pieces which are more mobile than the corresponding defending pieces on your side. At worst you will meet with immediate disaster. Two of your scattered pawns may be forked by an enemy piece so that one has to go; or one may be so awkwardly placed that you cannot protect it as much as your opponent can attack it, so that it falls into his hand like a ripe plum. You make this sort of thing easy for your opponent when you push pawns right under his nose.

Particularly dangerous is to advance the pawns in front of your king, whether he has remained in the centre or migrated, by castling, to a wing. *Never* move these pawns without good reason - if your opponent's pieces once get behind them, your king may be at his mercy. We have pointed out the danger of exposing him in a mêlée with the other pieces, for instance by moving him out, or even by leaving him, in the middle of the board. By moving away the pawns which originally screen him, you expose him almost as badly as if you were to push him out into the middle of the board. I once got hold of a very valuable chess book, published in 1562. Even at that early date they had discovered and mentioned this principle - but good players still lose games daily by forgetting it and unnecessarily moving the pawns that screen their king.

As pawns cannot move backwards, every pawn move is a permanent commitment. Like holy wedlock, you undertake it for better, for worse, for the remainder of the game. In the early stages, move no pawns except those you *must* in order to let the pieces out into play. Allow yourself two, or at most three, pawn moves among the first dozen moves you make. After that, always choose a piece move in preference to a pawn move unless the latter promises some lasting profit.

In two circumstances only can pawns be thrust well forward

without too much risk:

(a) When they advance in an unbroken line side by side, like infantry in a well-ordered attack. When this happens, they can seriously trouble your opponent by trapping his pieces within a more and more cramped space. The advancing line is called a 'pawn-roller'.

(b) When one or two can be thrust so far forward that there is a real threat that one will queen and, at the same time, can be adequately protected.

Both these are difficult operations, make no mistake! The first especially so; the advantage of controlling the greater area of the board can easily be over-estimated. Sooner or later the clash must come, when your line of pawns meets your opponent's. Two or three pawns on either side will be exchanged, files and diagonals being opened which were closed before, so that the pieces are suddenly freed. You should never allow this break-up to occur until you have carefully stationed all your pieces in readiness to take the fullest advantage of it - this will be easier for you that for your opponent as you have more room to manoeuvre in. If you neglect to do this, your opponent's pieces will become as mobile as your own and you will be the worse off because, by your general pawn-advance, you will have exposed your own king. Many first-rate players go astray

in this sort of position and it is instructive to observe the painstaking, almost fanatical caution with which a real master methodically crushes any attempt by his opponent to gain anything from the break-up. We shall soon explain why the pawns should advance in 'line abreast'.

The second case has not quite the same pitfalls. As we shall see later, there is a way of testing whether a pawn has a good chance of becoming a queen. Even in this instance, however, you may suddenly find your advanced pawn stuck, and becoming a liability instead of an asset, as hostile pieces fasten on to it one by one or make troublesome use of the square in front of it.

Pawn Formations: General

A pawn can rarely come to much harm if not too far advanced and protected by another pawn, the two occupying adjoining squares along the same diagonal as the black pawns in Diagram 48. Add a third pawn and a fourth along the same diagonal, and each protects the one before it, an extreme case of this being the black pawns in Diagram 99. This is a strong formation and a safe one, but safety tactics rarely pay so well as enterprise. The best defence is attack, and the best element in attack is mobility; the line of pawns straight across the board, as in Diagram 100, which we recommend above as a 'pawn-roller', is a superior formation, because it is more mobile and elastic.

Compare these two groups of four pawns, one in each formation:

Diagram 99
Safe (Diagonal) formation

Diagram 100
Mobile (Pawn-roller) formation

(a) How many pawns are protected at the moment? Of the 'safes', three; of the other, none.

The 'safes' win.

(b) How many pawns could acquire additional protection by a move, at need? Of the 'safes', none; of the 'rollers', any (by moving one square forward; either of the inner pawns so moved would immediately become doubly protected in this way). The 'rollers' are superior in this respect.

(c) How many squares are under control? (We found this a useful guide with the pieces.) A maximum of five in the 'safe', six in the 'roller' formation (we cannot count the square a pawn already stands on, because it is not available for any piece that might require protection).

Two of the 'rollers'' squares are protected twice over, so they win on this too.

(d) What happens if a pawn must move? In the case of the 'safes', the whole formation is broken up and at least one other pawn becomes unprotected. Again a win for the 'rollers', for 'roller' pawns actually gain protection when they move.

A further advantage of the second formation is that it sets up a barrier across the board just like the queen's barrier down the board in Diagram 36 (or the rook which could replace her). Every one of the squares in front of the line is under fire from a pawn, some twice over. An enemy king, coming from the front in Diagram 100, would be denied the use of the whole of the part of the board shown, except the top rank. If the king *cannot* approach, other pieces *dare not*. Preserve your pawn-roller intact whilst you can. When the time is ripe, move one pawn forward one square, then another, then a third each in turn taking up station one rank further forward, until the line is reformed on this rank and the enemy pieces are shut up into a still smaller part of the board than before.

It is found in practice that infiltration by enemy pieces is easier against the 'safe' formation.

Owing to its cramping effect on the enemy game and its elasticity, the 'roller' formation is better for all general circumstances.

The 'roller' formation is not chess for the lazy man; none of the pawns being protected, you must keep your wits about you in handling the 'roller', or you will lose pawns, but it is effective chess and, intelligently handled, will trouble any opponent far more than the easy-going 'safe' formation play.

Though the pawns occupy this formation at the commencement of the game, you will not often be able to preserve a pawn-roller right across the board - it takes eight moves a rank and you have to be very lucky or clever to keep your opponent quiet for eight moves at a time. The ideal is to get the two pawns which you are allowed to move out in the

opening stages to the fourth ranks and then start using your 'pieces'. See Diagram 131. If a third and fourth pawn can then join the pair in the middle, taking advantage of a 'jab' or two at hostile pieces in doing so, you have a menacing 'pawn roller' in the making.

Whenever you have the upper hand, or hold the initiative or are on the attack, try to get your pawns side by side on adjacent squares of one rank, as in Diagram 100. Look on the formation where one pawn protects another as a defensive resource to be adopted only in a sector where your opponent has the better of things. This applies to a pair of neighbouring pawns just the same as to a group of three or four or five. Needless to say, never stay on the defensive longer than you can help.

An 'Isolated' Pawn

Diagram 101

Look at this position: Black's pawns are in two groups of three. White's are grouped two, one and three. The one in the middle is a special kind of pawn; it is said to be 'isolated' because on each side of it is an open file - a file from which pawns of its own side have disappeared. Never could a *fellow-pawn* come to its rescue at the appointed station for protection (one square behind diagonally), if it were attacked it would have to call upon a *piece* for help. Because pawns can only move straight forwards except on those comparatively rare occasions where they make a capture, they cannot extend their help further away than the next file.

Is it good or is it bad, that this 'isolated' pawn might have to call upon pieces for protection? We have only to recall the battleship and the fishing vessel, to realise that it is bad. It is bad for a pawn to have to call on a piece to protect it. An isolated pawn is a weakness. Try to avoid isolating your own pawns and try to isolate your opponents.

Not only when attacked are the disadvantages of your isolated pawn made manifest. The square in front of him, the one on to which he would advance if he were to move, is a weak point in your game, a point of which your opponent can make good use for stationing his pieces. Why? Because (a) no *pawn* of yours can

attack a piece stationed there, as is obvious when we remember that you have no pawn on either of the adjacent files; and (b) of the *pieces* which might attack a hostile unit so stationed, the strongest, your queen and two rooks, would be unable to do so from the easiest direction - up the file - because your own file is in the way. Consequently that square is safer for an enemy man than it otherwise would be. If your opponent has an isolated pawn, try to work out which will benefit you more, to attack it so that you tie down his pieces to the defence of it, or to post a piece (a knight is usually best for this) on the square in front of it. If, in the latter case, your piece is captured, try to arrange recapture by a *piece*; recapturing with a pawn practically eliminates the isolated pawn's weakness. If you are unfortunate enough to get one of your own pawns isolated, try to exchange it off or to bring another of your pawns on to one of the files next to it, by means of a capture, so as to end its isolation.

A 'Doubled' Pawn

When two pawns belonging to the same side are on the same file, they are said to be 'doubled'. This, too is disadvantageous. The two pawns on the right in Diagram 102 are doubled. Their principal disadvantage in the early stages of the game is the fact that, instead of there being one pawn available on each side for protection in case of need (as there is for every pawn, except those on the extreme wings, in the position from which the game starts) there is now only one pawn available to protect the doubled two.

Diagram 102

If either of the doubled pawns be attacked, only one pawn is available to protect it - instead of the two there were originally. If the other doubled pawn be now attacked as well, it must seek protection from a piece. Bad! Also the two pawns on the same file get into each other's way - the hinder of those on the right in Diagram 102 cannot move at all. These disadvantages may be out-weighed, early on in a game, by the fact that, in becoming dou-bled, a pawn always opens a file; when a pawn makes a capture, it goes onto the next file, leaving its

original file 'open'.

Note White's doubled pawn, near his king. On to the resulting open file, he should get a rook as soon as possible, placing it where his king stands now.

Diagram 103

A rook is very happy if it has an open file, as we have indi-cated. Therefore, *early on*, it may benefit a player to double his pawns, as he can usually exploit his rooks well by playing them on to the open files thus created.

In the endgame, the rooks may have been exchanged off. Pawns will certainly have been ex-changed off, and there will be so many open files as a rule that one more or less will make little dif-ference. Then the doubled pawns become a weakness without any mitigating circumstances and, in a simple endgame with only kings or kings and one minor piece aside, the fact that you have doubled pawns whereas your op-ponent has not, may easily lose you the game. So if your opponent gets doubled (or isolated) pawns, try to exchange pieces off so as to speed progress to the endgame.

Rooks are much better than knights or bishops for exploiting these pawn weaknesses. If pawns of your own are doubled, try to make use of the open file or files created, to gain you some compensating advantage or - still better - to win the game altogether, before the endgame stage is reached. Or try to exchange off one of the doubled pawns.

When pawns are both doubled and isolated, as in the next diagram, they are very weak indeed. This pawn-formation could arise from White capturing a black knight and Black recapturing with the protecting pawn.

Diagram 104

If you acquire such a liability as doubled or isolated pawns (Diagram 104) your only hope is to create diversions in various parts of the board. Make it a 'scrappy' game; be ready to sacrifice material to expose your opponent's king; try for all you are worth to conjure up discovered checks, pins, forks, etc.

If the game takes a quiet course, your pawn-weakness will surely prove fatal in the end.

A 'Passed' Pawn

I said there was a way of testing whether a pawn had a good chance to queen, and here we are. A pawn is called 'passed' when there are no enemy pawns on the same file or on either of the two neighbouring files. The advanced white pawn in the middle of Diagram 105 is a 'passed' one.

Diagram 105

To realise why such a pawn is blessed to its possessor, and dangerous to his opponent, consider: how can a pawn, in general, prevent an enemy pawn from passing it? On the same file, by blocking it (as the bishop does in Diagram 10); on either of the adjacent files, by capturing it immediately it comes into range. A *passed* pawn cannot be hindered in either of these ways, so that *pieces* have to be deputed for the job and here we have a fishing vessel which makes the enemy employ a battleship to keep it harmless. Some fishing vessel!

When a pawn becomes 'passed', its chances of queening, and its value to its owner, rise with a jump.

If you allow one of your opponent's pawns to become 'passed', try to plant a piece securely on the square to which it is ready to advance. This operation is termed 'blockading' it. The best 'blockader' is a knight or a bishop, because the pawn it blockades does not interfere with its action. A queen or rook loses its forward power when used as a blockader and is also too valuable. Because it must move away when attacked by a minor piece or pawn, it is less effective in preventing the pawn's advance.

If the passed pawn is an isolated one, this blockade may become a nuisance to the pawn's possessor, as will be obvious from what we said under 'isolated pawns'. If it has a companion on an adjacent file, it is stronger because the companion might be able to come up and drive away the blockader; in Diagram 105

the hinder of White's two advanced pawns can 'raise the blockade' at once.

If that companion as well is a 'passed' pawn, they are said to be 'united passed pawns' and are a potent winning factor at any stage in any game.

Two united passed pawns on the sixth rank might even be stronger than a rook, if it cannot prevent one of them from queening. See Diagram 106.

Diagram 106

Set the men out like this on a board, take the pawns and get a friend to take the rook, giving him first move. Confirm that, wherever the rook goes and even if it attacks a pawn at once, one of the pawns can always queen. Whoever has the pawns must push them forward at every opportunity and must always be ready to allow one to be captured so as to queen the other. (This rule may of course not hold if a king is near enough to interfere.)

A 'Backward' Pawn

A pawn which has lagged a square or more behind its neighbours on either side is a 'backward' pawn and has some of the weaknesses of an isolated pawn.

Diagram 107

Diagram 108

See the middle pawn of Diagrams 107 and 108, and note how, just as if it were an isolated pawn, it cannot be protected, nor can the square in front of it be attacked, by any of its fellow-*pawns*; this square is called a 'hole' and a keen opponent will lose no opportunity of posting a minor piece there. A backward pawn is not quite as bad as an isolated pawn because (a) if it can advance, its weakness is completely eliminated and it becomes part of a good 'pawn-roller'; and (b) the friendly pawns ahead screen it from attack to some extent.

One Pawn Holding Two

Diagram 109

The diagram shows one particular situation in which a backward pawn can be disastrous. The one black pawn on the left prevents both opposing white pawns from moving; if the hinder (the 'backward' pawn) advances it can be captured and, though this frees the other, the black pawn queens first. White's extra pawn is useless and Black can draw easily.

The 'Pawn-Skeleton'

Your skeleton changes less than your flesh.

A fat man on a slimming diet can shed much fat in a few weeks, but his skeleton remains unaffected and his bones weigh the same before as after. A one-armed man might put on pounds of flesh but he could not grow a new arm. The pawns, because they move so slowly, form a sort of skeleton around which the whole game develops. Or, if you like, a slow changing maze, in whose open spaces, the livelier pieces play hide and seek - only occasionally trampling down the walls.

As a result of the contrast in the mobility of your pieces and your pawns, weaknesses in a player's position can be of two quite different types: (a) A 'positional' weakness or 'pawn-weakness'; or (b) a 'piece-weakness'. The most clean-cut example of the first is a doubled and isolated pawn; of the second, a piece placed in such a position that it could be captured for nothing. The greatest contrast is in 'time'; if your opponent were to overlook your blunder in case (b), you could undo all the harm by moving your piece away again, whereas only a big piece of luck could straighten out again your doubled and isolated pawns (yes, I know a suitable capture

could, but no opponent in his senses would lightly allow it).

Piece-weakness is a thing of the moment, soon rectified if the chance be allowed, but susceptible to drastic punishment, For examples look at Diagrams 61 to 63, where Black loses at least a rook for a knight. In either case, if he had placed his rook and queen or king on almost any other square, the white knight could not have 'forked' them. Look at Diagram 84, where White may lose his bishop if he leaves it undefended but can easily save it by withdrawing it. 'Creating a piece-weakness' might seem merely another name for 'making a blunder'. But look at Diagram 77, where White can win a piece through a piece-weakness, simply because Black's king, queen and knight happen to stand where they do. It might be too sweeping to say that Black had 'blundered' to allow White's very neat bit of play.

Piece-play and combination of the pieces are the very essence of chess. Only plenty of practice against many opponents will teach you the manifold possibilities of interplay of the pieces, but a few principles will help, as I shall show. Just now, it is with pawns that I am mainly concerned, and I want to emphasise that pawn-weaknesses are in some ways more important, as they are certainly more persistent, than piece-weaknesses. A pawn-weakness was described by one famous player as a 'chronic illness which, if you don't take drastic steps, will slowly but surely kill you'. As we have seen, they may persist and become increasingly troublesome as the game goes on - this very fact may force you to play the whole game in a way quite different from your original intention. If you have bad pawn-weaknesses, you must try to avoid exchanging pieces off; try to keep the game complicated, lively, double-edged, do all

you can to provoke 'piece-weaknesses' that may save you by leading to a sudden end. Obviously, if you can win a piece by a fork, or a pin, or a discovered check, you can sit back and laugh at an opponent whose only consolation is that one of your pawns is weakly placed; but his smile will become more and more smug if you mess about doing nothing in particular, whilst the effects of this weak placing become more and more serious.

7 The Pieces and the Pawns

The Pawn in the Endgame

In an endgame where all but a few of the pieces have been exchanged off, the pawns (and their strengths and weaknesses) gain immensely in importance. For instance, suppose one player is left with king and knight, the other with king and pawn. The knight could only win in a most exceptional case (a knight and a king alone cannot give mate), whereas the owner of the pawn might be able to promote it to queen which could checkmate even against the knight.

Kings and Pawns

To find whether a passed pawn can be caught in a king and pawn endgame before it succeeds in queening, imagine a square drawn on the board, one of whose sides is the path formed by the pawn going in to queen and which is on the same side of this path as the opposing king. If the opposing king is in this square or, having the move, can enter it,

then it can stop the pawn from queening, otherwise not.

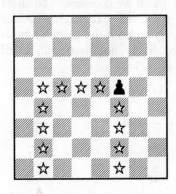

Diagram 110

Diagram 110 shows this imaginary 'queening-square'. Do not overlook the fact that, if the pawn stands on its original square, it could move two squares forward on its first move; the imaginary 'queening-square' must be formed as though the pawn stood one square in front of its real position, i.e. on its possessor's third rank (Diagram 111).

Again, if the other king is there to help the pawn in, it may be impossible to prevent the pawn queening. If a passed pawn has to be blockaded in an endgame, give the job to the king rather than any other piece; it is better to free the other piece for general duties than to assign these to the king.

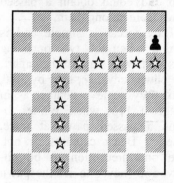

Diagram 111

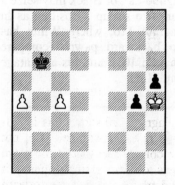

Diagram 112

A king can stop two united passed pawns but cannot capture either. They are 'self-protecting'. The typical position reached is shown on the right-hand side of Diagram 112, where the black pawns are coming down the board. the front pawn cannot be captured, being protected by its companion; whilst if the hinder one were captured, the other would immediately race forward to queen, the king being unable to catch it.

The pawns on the left of Diagram 112 are similarly 'self-protecting', as can be verified by trial. If the black king plays on to the square in front of one of them, threatening it, the other advances and then, if Black captures, can go on to queen.

The 'Distant' Passed Pawn

When each side has a passed pawn in a king-and-equal-pawns-only endgame, the advantage belongs to the player whose passed pawn is further from his opponent's king. A clean-cut example of this is shown in Diagram 113. The position looks even, but White has an easy win because he has the 'distant' or 'remote' passed pawn. He pushes it forwards two or three squares; the black king must, willy-nilly, cross the board to stop and capture it and, because it is so far away, White has time to capture first Black's passed pawn and then the remaining black pawns before the black king can get back. With his two remaining pawns, White then wins easily.

Though a distant passed pawn is a useful weapon in most circumstances, it is a deadly winning factor when the slow-moving kings are the only pieces left; if your opponent has one, avoid exchanging off the last piece at all costs.

Diagram 113

The 'Queenside Pawn Majority'

When, on one side of the board, you have more pawns than your opponent, you can usually obtain a passed pawn there.

Diagram 114

In Diagram 114 there is a completely open file near the middle. On the left of this, White has three pawns to his opponent's two and could obtain a passed pawn from among them.

The process is simple and is similar when the two opposing sets of pawns start further apart; the pawns advance, side by side, until they achieve contact as in Diagram 115, when White obtains a passed pawn at once, whether Black captures or not. The one precaution to be observed is 'never to let the pawn which has no enemy pawn directly facing it lag behind its neighbours', or Black may seize a chance to set up a position as in Diagram 116, where White has two backward pawns (compare Diagram 109), and his advantage is nullified.

Diagram 115

On the right-hand side of Diagram 114, Black has four pawns to White's three and could thus obtain a passed pawn himself on this side. You might think the chances are equal, but they are not - they are in White's favour because *his* passed pawn will be a 'distant' one.

Diagram 116

In most games each player 'castles' with the rook nearer his king, i.e. White on his right, Black on the same side of the board (his left). Consequently, whoever obtains a majority of pawns on the opposite side of the board - the 'queenside', as we explain elsewhere - obtains also a potential 'distant passed pawn' and has thus secured a subtle but real positional advantage. A 'queenside pawn majority' is also extremely useful before the endgame is reached and whilst there are still a few pieces on each side not exchanged off. Whoever possesses it, can push forward his pawns to make a passed pawn without undue anxiety, whereas his opponent will have to be cau-

tious because the pawns he must advance are those screening his own king, which may become exposed in consequence.

Do you follow this? To have a majority of pawns on the wing distant from the kings is good because you can advance the pawns without fear of exposing your king in the process, and because the passed pawn eventually obtained from them will be a 'distant' one.

Doubled pawns have a curious effect. They minimise all the advantage of a pawn majority, for it is hardly ever possible to produce a passed pawn out of a pawn majority containing them; but in defence they are quite good. Thus in Diagram 117, Black has a clear advantage; White's 3 to 2 majority on the left or 'queenside' will be useless, whereas Black's majority on the opposite wing will duly produce a passed pawn.

Diagram 117

The best attempt White can make is to arrive at a position like Diagram 118, when Black moves his attacked pawn one square and White can get nowhere.

Diagram 118

Knights and Pawns

If you are trying to protect a lone pawn with a lone knight, against a lone king, get the knight *behind* the pawn. Then if the knight is captured, the pawn can queen.

Diagram 119

Whereas in Diagram 126, where Black (playing *down* the board) has mistakenly protected his pawn from in front, White has time to capture first knight and then pawn.

Rooks and Pawns

A good rule, whenever you are concerned mainly with rooks and pawns, is to post the rook if possible *behind* a pawn, i.e. so that the pawn, if moved, goes away from it. This applies in all parts of the game, equally for attack and defence, whether the rook and the pawn belong to the same player or not.

Rook and pawn *v.* rook (plus kings, of course) is a common ending which illustrates the rule perfectly.

Diagram 120

In Diagram 120, as long as the black rook can stay where it is, it will blockade the white pawn, which is striving to go up the board to queen. *But* if Black should have to move his rook, it must give way step by step, until finally, when it gets to Black's back rank, it cannot move at all without allowing the pawn to queen. Meanwhile the white rook has freedom of action behind the pawn, being able to move to any square on the file and still protect the pawn and threaten its advance; freedom of action which increases with every successive advance the pawn makes.

and down the file it stands on. The white king can render no effective assistance since, directly it approaches his pawn so as to protect it and release his rook, the black rook can drive him away by a series of checks from the distance (from which he can never escape as there is absolutely no shelter for him, owing to the placing of his rook and pawn) returning to the pawn's file as soon as the white king is once again out of touch with the pawn.

Diagram 121

Diagram 122

In Diagram 121 the positions are reversed. White can play his rook to the far edge of the board and advance the pawn after it to within one square of queening. Now he is stuck; he cannot move the pawn and any move of his rook leaves the pawn unprotected so it can be taken. (See Diagram 122).

Black can safeguard the draw by simply moving his rook up

This helplessness of the white king, after the pawn is advanced to the seventh rank, teaches us a lesson. White should not advance his pawn quite so far, but should stop it one square short of its position in Diagram 122; this leaves an empty square between the white rook and the white pawn and if the white king can take refuge there from the black rook's distant checks, the pawn can often be queened in a few moves.

If the rook is best placed behind the passed pawn, the opposite is true of the king, which is usually of more use in front of the pawn. In fact, the great majority of rook-and-pawn versus rook endings depend on whether the defending king can get in front of the pawn. If he can, the game is frequently drawn. If it cannot, it is almost certainly lost.

The most common type of ending is that in which each side has king, one rook and several pawns. In this ending, the golden maxim is 'Use the rook for attack, not defence.' If your opponent should threaten to take one of your pawns, either defend with a pawn or your king or - often best - counter-attack one of your opponent's pawns with your own rook, using the rook for defence only in the last resort. Occasionally it may pay to defend with a rook, as a strictly temporary measure, until another man can relieve him. Utilise the rook's 'barrier' as much as possible, cutting off the hostile king from critical areas of the board altogether when you can.

Get your rook *behind* any passed pawn nearing its queening square. It is often more urgent that the king hurry to the critical scene of affairs than the rook; the latter, by virtue of its greater mobility, can usually come at once when required, but the slower king has to make an early start.

Bishops and Pawns

Diagram 123

Diagram 123 shows an obvious example of the effect of pawns on a bishop which has been trapped by them and is lost. *Mobile* pawns can usually disconcert an opposing bishop most by working on squares of the same colour as he occupies (as here). You will have to keep the situation well under control, for if they can attack him, he can attack them! As long as they remain mobile, they can always take refuge on opposite-coloured squares, where they are safe, when counter-attacked.

When the pawn situation is blocked, the whole situation may be reversed and it is usually fatal to have pawns fixed on squares where they are vulnerable to an enemy bishop.

There is no saving the black pawns in Diagram 131; the

bishop simply chews them up.

Diagram 124

'Good' and 'Bad' Bishop

We can regard this last position from another angle, taking it for granted that the pawns are blocked and assessing the merits of the bishop in the light of this fact. Obviously the bishop in Diagram 124 is a good useful piece. If he were a black-square bishop, however, he would be useless; his own pawns would get in his way, and against the enemy pawns he could do nothing.

If a game becomes blocked, the pawns must have congregated, one side's on white squares, the other side's on black. If one player's white-square bishop is a *good* piece, his opponent's white-square bishop is a *bad* one.

When two bishops are exchanged off, they are almost invariably those moving on similarly coloured squares; a white-square bishop can be exchanged for a black-square bishop only in some roundabout way since, obviously, one can never capture the other.

Diagram 125

What seems a humdrum exchange of bishop for bishop may be in reality the exchange of a useful piece for a useless one, and benefit one of the players a lot.

For instance, if the two bishops moving on white squares in Diagram 125 were removed, White would have an easy win. Remove the other two bishops instead, and Black should win. Obviously this is no unimportant consideration, though it may seem a little involved perhaps at first reading.

The Helpless Bishop with the Rook's Pawn

Diagram 126 is perhaps the most striking illustration of the bishop's one weakness. White is a bishop and a pawn to the good but cannot win - he must concede a draw, Black is stalemated as he stands and if White retreats his king, the black king comes out, only to bob back again next move. Black's salvation is the fact that his king can never be attacked on a *black* square. Neither the bishop nor the pawn (now that the latter is on a white square) can ever do so and, of course, the white king cannot, by the rules of the game.

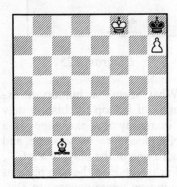

Diagram 126

The necessary conditions for this peculiar draw are: the pawn must be on one of the rook's files (the files at the extreme edge of the board); the defending king must be able to reach, and the bishop must be unable to command, its queening square. If one of these conditions fails, there is no draw; the owner of the pawn can win.

Trapping a 'Pawn-Snatcher'

An extremely common interplay of bishops and pawns is shown in Diagram 127.

Diagram 127

One of Black's pawns is attacked by the bishop and unprotected; but it would be fatal for White to capture it for then the next pawn would move one square forward - and the bishop would be trapped; the black king could come up and capture it.

8 How to Make Good Moves

The Importance of the Centre

Every piece is most effective in the centre of the board and least effective on the edges. Queen, bishop or rook can cross a clear board from side to side in one leap; but the board never is clear and, in the vast majority of cases when a piece is urgently required at a particular spot, it will have to evade or overcome one or more obstacles on the way there. A piece stationed on a wing may be too late for operations on the opposite side of the board. Its very absence from the centre is an invitation to your opponent to start an action on the opposite wing, where, through having disposed his forces more centrally, he may be able to bring an extra piece into the battle at the crucial moment.

With every succeeding year in the long history of chess, the profound importance of the centre has been more and more clearly recognised. The course of every game hinges on the situation on the four central squares. Nim-zowitsch of Riga, the 'stormy petrel' of the chess-world, who flatly contradicted his predecessors on so many points, could not contradict them on this, in fact went even further than they, maintaining that the centre is of paramount importance.

Especially should knights never be allowed to stray far from the centre, owing to the shortness of their stride, as well as to the way in which they are cramped by the edges of the board (page 37).

Diagram 128

The same applies to pawns with their even shorter stride. Often you are offered the alternative of making the same capture with either of two pawns. When this happens, unless there are definite reasons against it, you should capture with the pawn which, in so doing, moves towards the centre. (See the diagrams.) White can capture the bishop with either of two pawns.

Diagram 129
Position after capture towards centre (usually good).

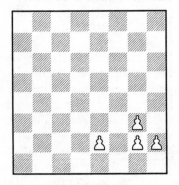

Diagram 130
Position after capture away from centre (usually bad).

Stressing the importance of the centre does not mean that you should place all your pieces there; this would produce a solid block of men which might badly hamper each other. It does mean that you should continually direct the action of your pieces towards the four critical centre squares and keep them all as near to the centre as you can, consistent with their interfering as little as possible with each others' freedom.

How to Play the Opening

A piece is far more mobile than a pawn. A rook can go as far in one move as a pawn in five. Consequently it is dangerous to utilise too many of your turns for pawn moves; particularly in the opening stages. Whilst you are laboriously pushing on your pawns one square at a time, your opponent's pieces, if he plays well, will flash in and among them and do irremediable damage. Some pawn moves you must naturally make as, with the pawns on a solid line in their original rank, only your knights could come out; you should keep pawn moves to a minimum, however, for at least the first nine or ten moves, moving only so many pawns as you must to let all the pieces out. As a rule, two pawn moves out of the first eight you make are sufficient and three are the most that you should ever allow yourself.

As a general rule you should

bring out first one or two pawns, then your knights, then your bishops; then you should castle and advance your queen a little; lastly bring your rooks to the middle of your back rank. 'Never move any piece twice, until you have moved every piece once,' is an old-fashioned maxim for the opening which has much to recommend it. Find a good square for each of your pieces in turn, where it causes your opponent as much trouble as possible; having placed it there, leave it for time being unless it is attacked or indirectly threatened; then turn to another piece and find a good square for that. Beginners are often fatally tempted to move one piece here, there and everywhere over the board without bringing the others out at all. This is clearly a mistaken policy, for no one piece can be so wonderfully well-placed that it is as good as four or five hostile pieces 'all' fairly well-placed - however many times you move it, it can only end up on one square from which it radiates one set of powers, whereas lines of effect from the more numerous hostile pieces will criss-cross the board like lines of fire from machine guns, soon rendering it dangerous for your remaining pieces to venture out at all. Look at Diagram 58, where a queen is helpless against a rook and a bishop - because there is only one of her!

'Ideal' Development

The following diagram is the most important in this book. It represents the ideal position you reach if your opponent allows you to play all the moves recommended above. Set up the pieces as for the start of the game and confirm that, moving the various pieces in the order suggested, they can produce this position in ten moves.

Diagram 131

Diagram 131 reveals the ideal development of the men in which they interfere least with each other's action but command the biggest number of important squares. But note the word 'ideal'. What is an 'ideal'? Something always worth striving for, but rarely attainable. This ideal position is like that. Not in one game out of a hundred will you be able to obtain it unhindered, because you have an opponent busy foiling your plans. If he were so stupid as to allow you to obtain that ideal position, he would have a terribly difficult game. He would even have to be very unlucky, not to make at least one move which unintentionally compelled some modification of your plans. Usually he will make several. You will usually be able to place your two knights, your queen, king and rooks on their 'ideal' squares. Your bishops may meet with trouble but the fact that each has a good alternative post (as explained under (a) below) will help. You will often have trouble with your pawns and may have to postpone bringing the second up abreast of the first. For example, suppose you play out the pawn in front of your queen two squares first move, and your opponent answers with a similar move.

Diagram 132

If you now play out the second pawn unthinkingly to produce Diagram 132, your opponent can capture it with his.

Yours is undefended; you cannot recapture so you have lost a pawn for nothing. In such a situation as this, you must substitute some other move of the plan, always seeking for a chance to get back to the plan in its purest form later on. Sometimes you will have to put up with moving one of your men to an obviously inferior square, so as to proceed towards the ideal with other moves which could not be made until this man is moved somewhere.

White has the advantage of the first move and can usually get nearer to the ideal than Black, who will have to be satisfied with more makeshift and inferior alternatives.

Just for Variety...

You can allow yourself two departures from this development.

(a) Either of the two bishops can go out one square further away from his original station if he can thus usefully pin a hostile knight as in Diagrams 83 and 84.

(b) You can add one more pawn to your central 'pawn-roller' by playing out either of the pawns behind your knights in Diagram 131 to a square there occupied by a bishop; this extra pawn move must be made before that knight comes out - obviously

- and the bishop which would have occupied that square must, if it cannot travel (along its diagonal) one square beyond, stop one square short.

I strongly advise you not to bother about (b) until you have played numerous games based on Diagram 131 with (a) as the one and only luxury departure permitted. The extra pawn move in (b) is justified by the grip you get on the central squares but leads to a quieter, more difficult and possibly less enjoyable game.

The Weaver Adams Method

Naturally at every move of every game you play, you must make sure that you are not committing some elementary blunder such as leaving a piece where it can be taken - this is obvious. Moreover, at every move you should make as exact and deep a calculation as you can to determine what your opponent's most likely reply move will be, how you will answer it, and so on. When calculation reveals clearly that you can win a piece, or may lose a piece, or mate your opponent's king, or something equally drastic, your line of action is clearly indicated, but in the vast majority of cases, decisive 'combinations' like these will be lacking and you will be adrift on an immense sea of possibilities. Many great players have attempted to supply a rudder

for your boat and of these I think that of a well-known American player, Weaver Adams, is simplest.

He holds that four things are worth striving for: Power, Mobility, Options, and the avoidance of Weaknesses. P, M, O, W! Learn these four letters and you will rarely forget what they stand for (I found them easier to remember as a pronounceable word 'POWM').

Power. Easy! The more squares and the more important squares a piece commands, or the more important the hostile men it attacks, the greater is its power. Try to place pieces on squares where they are most effective, i.e. most powerful.

Your men gain in power as they *advance* closer to important enemy units (these two statements are amply exemplified by the cocky little pawn in Diagram 42, which by throwing itself at the enemy king, has won the game).

A cruder aspect of power, but one which it is possible to forget in abstractions, is the fact that - a pawn is a pawn, and a bishop is a bishop! To have won one of your opponent's pawns is a solid achievement and has in itself brought you nearer to victory. As a rule beginners find it much more difficult to appreciate positional factors such as well-placed pieces, an exposed king, and such like, than material factors such as the loss of a piece or pawn; so all elementary text books deliberately stress the former at the expense of the latter. Occasionally they swing the pendulum too far, and the learner acquires a mistaken disdain of material power; he gets into the habit of sacrificing a pawn or a piece for almost nothing. A positional advantage is not an advantage at all until you have learnt what to do with it; and my considered advice (which I should be prepared to argue out with anybody though it runs contrary to the general run of text-book instruction) is to husband your men pretty parsimoniously until you have begun to 'get the feel of them' and have had a few chances to exploit positional advantages whilst free from disturbing nervous tension engendered by starting the whole operation a piece or a pawn to the bad. Otherwise, whilst your games may be bold, original and interesting, you may lose far too many.

A pawn's a pawn, for a' that!

Mobility. Nor is this difficult. A man is well-placed where he has freedom of action, badly placed when he is hampered and cramped by other men, whether friends or foes. The effect of lack of mobility can be drastic, as Diagram 133 illustrates. Here White, with rook against knight, would normally win. But he actually loses on account of the lack of mobility of his rook, which,

impeded by the pawns, cannot be saved from the attack of the knight.

Diagram 133

Remember to consider the mobility of other men besides the one moved.

Diagram 134

For instance, White decides, in Diagram 134, to develop his bishop. It would actually have the greatest mobility on the square marked with an 'X', from which it could move off again to any of ten different squares; but on that square it would rob the white rook of access to five important squares. A better square for it is the one marked with a circle where, though it has not quite the same mobility itself, it does not detract from the mobility of any friendly piece.

Options. It pays to conserve valuable options until you are in a position to make the best use of them. For instance, one of your pieces might have the option of moving in either of two ways, each of which might cause your opponent trouble. Either of these might be a better move than any other you could make, but it might yet pay to hold the option in reserve for the moment, to keep your opponent on tenterhooks. Perhaps on the very next turn to play, you may find that one of them now wins outright - you would feel silly if you had made the other, and achieved nothing by it!

Conversely, if there is any move you obviously *must* make sooner or later, it usually pays to do it at once, otherwise you might have to make it later on when you would desperately like to make another. In doing this you will be conserving optional moves.

Weaknesses. This should be clear. A move, however good in other respects, might have to be avoided if it creates a weakness in your game, or allows your opponent to force one.

These four factors must be weighed up one against the other and also considered from your opponent's point of view. Thus if you can force weaknesses, or restrict the mobility of his men or rob them of some or part of their power, you are doing just as well as you would be registering positive improvements in your own P, M, O, W factors.

Thus, turn to Diagram 134 again. In that position, the black bishop is pinned (confirm this). If White moves his bishop to the square marked with an 'X', he *unpins* the black bishop, i.e. releases it for the pin, enabling this piece which previously could not move at all, to go on at will to any of the five different squares. On one of these squares, White's queen stands, and could now be captured! We see that a wretchedly bad move might be made, quite unsuspectingly, through failing to take the wide view. Consider your forces as a whole!

Consider the situation frequently and habitually from your opponent's view as well as your own. Whilst waiting for him to move, rise from your seat and (all this as unobtrusively as possible, of course) go round behind him and have a quiet look at the game from his side. You may see at a glance strengths or weaknesses in his game you had not previously suspected. Watch his demeanour - a worried look may reveal that he has difficulties you had not noticed.

Above all, keep an *elastic* outlook. Those P, O, M, W factors are to be considered only in the light of every other possibility.

In Diagram 135, White's obvious selection for either Power or Mobility would be a move with his rook on to one of the open files. This would give the rook seven more squares to operate on than he has now. But the serious weakness this would allow Black to force by taking the knight next move, saddling White, on recapturing, with doubled and isolated pawns, compels postponement of the rook move in favour of moving the knight so as to avoid this capture.

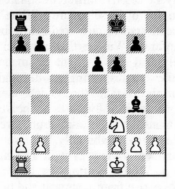

Diagram 135

In another case, the opposite might hold; it might be worthwhile submitting to a small permanent weakness to seize the chance of getting in a move which represents a great increment of power.

The Weaver Adams formula applies whenever clean-cut combinations are not discernible.

If at first it seems a bit hazy to you, or you cannot see exactly how it works, don't worry; use it as you play actual games and you will gradually realise what a help it can be.

Even a sketchy understanding of the principles outlined in this book will give you an immense advantage over the 'natural' player and after a few dozen games you may find yourself beating people who have played chess half a lifetime.

Some Random Good Advice

Never forget you have an opponent and become so engrossed in your own plans that you overlook what he is up to. Always ask yourself, when your opponent makes a move 'Why did he do that?' You may find you can ignore his threats for the moment; on the other hand, you may have to attend to them at once.

Don't let your opponent distract you by trivial offers. After you have won a pawn, even if the position is otherwise even, you are still a long way from a win, whereas, if your pieces are well and powerfully placed, you can often crash through to victory quickly. Develop your pieces to good squares, *then* begin to think of capturing material!

Having decided on your move and when just about to make it, take a quick glance round the board to make sure you are not committing some simple blunder, leaving a piece to be captured for nothing, or overlooking something urgent.

Don't play too many games in succession, especially if you are losing them and becoming discouraged.

Always try to play against someone slightly better than yourself. Hard on your opponent, of course; you will sometimes have to diverge from this plan out of politeness. But what a golden maxim this is in any game.

Whilst waiting for your opponent to decide on his move, don't gaze vacantly into space. Don't, on the other hand, go into a maze of vague complications on the board - calculations which can have little value if your opponent has (as is often the case) a dozen good possible moves at his disposal.

Do examine the position in a detached sort of way from time to time for *general* characteristics you may have overlooked in your previous precise analysis. See if the last few moves have introduced some unexpected factor into the position which you may both have overlooked.

Three things besides 'forks', 'skewers', 'pins', 'over-burdened pieces', etc. to seek for are:

(a) Unguarded, or insufficiently guarded pieces;

(b) Discovered attacks, similar to discovered checks (page 30), where you uncover an attack from one of your men by moving another; and

(c) Possible weaknesses.

Play a free, open game. If you have just moved a man, that in itself is usually a good reason for not moving it again for a while. Use *all* your forces, not just a part of them.

To begin with, you will win quite a number of games by simply taking advantage of glaring blunders on the part of your opponent - you may attack a piece and he may altogether overlook your attack, allowing you to capture it for nothing. You will not get far like this, however, and should always strive to delve as deeply into the position as possible.

Always have some definite aim. If anybody were to ask you, at any time 'Why did you make that move?' you should always be able to give an answer.

Given two moves start, a master could win every game. Time is an all-important factor. You can waste time by bringing out your queen too early in the fray, so that your opponent can bring out one minor piece after another, attacking her; all she can do is to move away from the attack each time, whilst your opponent is mobilising his whole army, man by man. You can *gain* time by finding useful moves for yourself which compel your opponent to make useless ones.

Time is such an important factor that it is considered bad to win a pawn if it takes more than three moves to do so. The pawn is just not worth the time wasted which your opponent, if he knows his business, may utilise to move three more pieces into threatening positions from which they can deliver a telling blow.

Remember Weaver Adams' four points, especially Power, Mobility and Weakness. Play your men to squares where they are as powerful as possible. Avoid weaknesses in your own game. Conversely, try to prevent your opponent's men from getting to good squares; try to cramp his game and create and exploit weaknesses among his men.

It is the *geography* of a position which counts, not its *history*. If you have been on the defence for an hour or more, that is no reason for remaining on the defensive if your opponent allows you an opening for an attack. Don't let depression affect your keenness. Conversely if you have been attacking brilliantly that is no reason for continuing the attack if the best the situation can really offer is to gain a safe pawn and transpose into a won endgame.

When, and When Not, to Exchange

You will frequently be offered the chance to take a knight in return for a knight of your own, or a pawn for a pawn, or a queen for a queen, or so on. This is called 'exchanging' and it is not always easy to decide whether it is advisable or not.

Every exchange of *pieces* brings you nearer to the endgame, consequently you should welcome exchanges if, on the whole, you are well-placed for the endgame, and fight shy of them if not. Pawn exchanges favour a drawn result, so they are welcome when you are fighting to avoid loss.

In general, it is strongly advisable to seize every safe chance of exchanging pieces when (a) you are materially to the good, e.g. a pawn up; 2-1 is better odds than 3-2; or (b) you are in a cramped position; for when you have only a few squares at your disposal, the fewer pieces there remain to use them, the less you feel the shortage.

Conversely, if you have the freer game or are material down, you should avoid exchanging pieces as a rule.

Other obviously advantageous exchanges are (a) when the enemy man is better placed than yours; (b) when the exchange creates a weakness in your opponent's position or eliminates one from yours; or (c) when you 'gain time' by exchanging.

If you are under attack, you can often relieve the pressure by exchanges; an exchange of queens is particularly efficacious, often robbing an attack of its sting.

As a general rule, when you cannot make up your mind at all, exchange! To go out of your way to avoid exchanging may mean to waste time and fritter away an initiative.

Castling

I am often asked for advice on how and when to castle. A safe general rule is: 'Castle as early as convenient, on the kingside.' Very occasionally, it pays to castle on the queenside, usually with a view to leaving one's back-rank kingside squares vacant for use by pieces engaged in a direct attack on an opposing king which has castled on the kingside. Still more rarely, it pays to postpone castling deliberately, retaining the option of castling either side so that your opponent is kept in doubt how to dispose his pieces for the eventual assault. In general, avoid castling when your opponent has an open file or diagonal bearing on to one or more of the pawns which would be in front of your (castled) king. In nine cases out of ten, however, you should castle pretty early, on the kingside.

9 Chess Notation

How to Record Games

When you read newspaper or magazine columns you will encounter weird-looking symbols such as ♘f3 and ♕xf7+, etc. These are examples of the notation by which the moves of a game of chess can be recorded and preserved, in the same way as the notes and chords of a piece of music. A chess master plays a game; a musician plays a tune. In each case the beauty can be preserved on paper, so that, in the one case it can be conjured up again by means of a chessboard and men, in the other by a piano.

Understanding of the system of notation is not absolutely essential to an enjoyment of chess, but it opens up such a fairyland of delight that no chess player can be excused for failing to learn it early in his career. The symbols enable you to crystallise your ideas, impressions and opinions, and to delve easily into the richness of the vast literature of chess. Every book on chess employs notation of some kind, and the standard form used nowadays throughout the world is known as 'algebraic' notation. Don't be put off if you were not too hot on algebra at school, there is little more involved in this notation than there is in reading an A-Z street map!

First, each piece is represented by a symbol as follows:

King: ♔
Queen: ♕
Rook: ♖
Bishop: ♗
Knight: ♘

No symbol is used for a pawn.

Diagram 135

So much for the pieces. The

squares on which they travel are identified by simple grid references. Thus if we take an empty board (Diagram 135) the square at the bottom left is a1, the square above that a2, the next going up a3 and so on until we get to the top left-hand square (a8). Moving to the second file along from the left, this is known as the b-file and contains the squares from b1 (at the bottom) to b8 (at the top). Moving along from the left it should now be easy to identify the c-file, d-file, e-file, f-file, g-file and h-file. You will notice that the bottom right-hand square is h1 and the top right h8. All that remains now is to put the symbols for the pieces together with the squares. Thus in the next diagram if White opens with 1 e4 (each move is preceded by the number of that move) then we see that his pawn moves from its original position two squares forward.

If Black were to reply 1 ... ♘f6 then the following position would be reached, with the white pawn having moved from e2 to e4 and the black knight from g8 to f6.

Diagram 137

Now let us say that White defended his pawn by moving his knight from b1 to c3, written as 2 ♘c3, and Black responded by advancing the pawn in front of his queen two squares forward: 2 ... d5. We would now reach the following position.

Diagram 136

Diagram 138

If White were to exchange pawns here, this would be written as 3 exd5, the piece or pawn making the capture is identified, a capture sign (x) inserted, and the square on which the capture is made identified.

Really that is all there is to algebraic notation. On occasion you may find that two white knights, for example, might be able to travel to the same square, in which case they are distinguished by the addition of the file on which they started off, e.g. ♘fd4 or ♘bd4, or if they start on the same file, the number of the rank they depart from is used instead, e.g. ♘2d4 or ♘6d4.

Other symbols are often used as standard abbreviations:

+	Check
!	Good move
!!	Brilliant move
?	Bad move
??	Blunder
!?	Interesting move
?!	Dubious move
ep	en passant
=	The position is equal
∞	The position is unclear
±	White stands slightly better
±	White stands much better
+−	White is winning
∓	Black stands slightly better
∓	Black stands much better
−+	Black is winning

Now let us examine two complete (albeit very short) games in algebraic notation. Usually White's moves are printed in a vertical column on the left and Black's in another column on the right. Even if there are whole paragraphs of notes and comments between the moves, you can always see whether a move is one of White's or Black's by observing whether it is placed to the right or the left of the column of print. First, a ridiculous game (the shortest possible) in which White commits suicide.

1   f3

White moves the pawn in front of his king's bishop forward one square.

1   ...   e6

This is a move by Black, of course, since it is printed to the right of the column of print. Black moves the pawn in front of his king forward one square.

2   g4??   ♕h4 mate

Diagram 139

Verify that White is now mated. His king is attacked by the queen, he cannot take the queen or interpose one of his own men in between her and his king; he cannot move his king to f2 since the queen could still capture him there; and he cannot move the king to any of the other four squares next to him on the board because they are each occupied by one of his own men. Next we shall give another brief game which illustrates the danger a beginner must avoid.

1   e4

This is one of the two very best moves which White can make to open the game. It at once frees the way for either his queen or his king's bishop (on f1) to come into action; and it presses on to squares in the centre of the board, which are most important, as we have already seen.

1   ...   e5

Probably Black's best response, for much the same reasons.

2   ♗c4   d6

3   ♕h5

Not really a good move, for the queen is too valuable a piece to throw into the game at such an early stage; but it does threaten something very unpleasant which Black overlooks here.

3   ...   ♘c6??

This is often an excellent move, but not here.

4   ♕xf7 mate

This mate (shown in Diagram 140) is known as fool's (scholar's) mate and you should learn how to avoid it. Actually it

is quite simple. Go back to the second move (after 1 e4 e5 2 ♗c4) and play 2 ... ♘f6. This is an excellent move for Black in ninety-nine games out of a hundred and you should always make it at an early stage unless there is a powerful reason why not to. Now White cannot play 3 ♕h5 as you would capture the queen and 3 ♕f3 does not threaten the f-pawn, because the way is blocked by the knight.

Diagram 140

In the rest of this book, algebraic notation is freely used. You should practice it and use it in your own games, particularly if you are playing against the clock and require a record of the number of moves that have been played. Much pleasure and instruction can be gained by playing your games over again afterwards and rejoicing over your brilliancies or finding where you went wrong.

10 Basic Endgame Motifs

Now we can tackle some topics which would have been difficult to explain before we understood the notation.

The Opposition

Diagram 141

This looks an even position, but *if it is Black's turn to move, White can win.* All the pawns are blocked and immovable, so that only the king can move for the moment; and however Black moves his king, he cannot prevent White's king thereupon advancing on to a black square beside one of the black pawns, and capturing that pawn next move. If the black king retreats to the right, the white one advances to the left, and *vice versa*. The win might come as follows:

1	...	♚e6
2	♔c5	♚d7
3	♔xb5	♚d6
4	♔b6	♚d7
5	b5	♚d8
6	♔a7	

and Black cannot prevent the white pawn queening within three moves.

Or:

4	...	♚d5
5	b5	♚e4
6	♔a6	♚xf4
7	b6	

and the white pawn queens in two more moves, whereas Black requires five (one with the king, to get out of the way of the pawn, and four with the pawn).

On the other hand, if it is White's turn to move it is he who must retreat (as is obvious) and he cannot possibly win unless Black makes some bad blunder. This illustrates the 'opposition', a relative situation of the two kings which enables the one who has *not* to move to make ground towards the other.

Diagram 142

Diagram 143

Diagram 144

The two basic 'opposition' positions are shown in diagrams 142 and 143. To have to move in either of those positions is to have to give ground.

An interesting extension of the idea is shown in Diagram 144, where, whoever has to move must eventually give ground, because, whatever forward move he makes, his opponent can 'gain the opposition' by setting up a position such as Diagram 141. Suppose it is White's turn. If he plays 1 ♔e3, Black replies 1 ... ♚e5; if he plays 1 ♔d3, Black replies 1 ... ♚d5. On 1 ♔c3 comes 1 ... ♚c5. In each case, White on his next move must give way and allow Black to advance, capture a pawn first, and win. Whenever an odd number of squares separates the kings (here *one* in Diagram 141 and *three* in Diagram 144), whoever moved last has set up the opposition and his opponent, as a result of the necessity to move, must sooner or later give ground.

The effect of the opposition disappears if moves are available by other pieces or pawns, but it is powerful (and can decide the result of the game, as we have seen) when only king moves are possible.

Queening a Sole Surviving Pawn

Here is a typical and important example of the opposition

(Diagram 145). Obviously White is striving to force his pawn onwards to the back rank to promote it to a queen and then win. Black is trying to prevent this and, if he should succeed, would draw the game. Whoever can 'gain the opposition' achieves his aim. If it is White's move he plays **1 ♔f6** and can win. Black can only, in reply, move to e8 or g8.

Diagram 145

If he goes to e8, White plays 2 ♔g7; if he goes to g8, White plays 2 ♔e7. In either case Black can do nothing thereafter to prevent the pawn marching straight through to promotion. Note that, after 1 ♔f6, White would be 'no forrarder' if only Black were not compelled to move; the white king could not advance to any of the three squares in front of him for they are all guarded by the black king. Black, simply because he has to move, must give up control of one of them and

allow White to push ahead.

Suppose it is Black's move, instead of White's, in the diagrammed position. Now *he* can seize the opposition and doing so is enough, with care subsequently, to secure him the draw: **1 ... ♔g7!**. The play is a little more complicated but the following possible sequels show how Black has always a defence if he takes care to keep the opposition and never allows White to gain the opposition against him.

(a) **2 f6+ ♔f7 3 ♔f5 ♔f8! 4 ♔g6 ♔g8 5 f7+ ♔f8 6 ♔f6.**

Any other legal move would allow Black to capture the pawn but this puts him in stalemate. Drawn game! Had Black moved 3 ... ♔g8? instead of 3 ... ♔f8 he would have lost: **4 ♔g6 ♔f8 5 f7 ♔e7** (the only move) **6 ♔g7** and White queens the pawn next move.

Often it is given as a maxim that the defender can always secure his heaven-sent stalemate in this sort of ending if the pawn *gives check* to him as it gets to the seventh rank; if the pawn gets safely on to the seventh without checking him, as in the last line of play shown, he is lost. But this is only another way of saying that he is safe whilst he keeps the opposition, for the pawn can only get safely on to the seventh rank without checking him if he has lost the opposition. Verify this.

Now to examine another line of play which might arise from

the diagrammed position after Black's initial 1 ... ♔g7!:

(b) **2 ♔h5 ♔f6** (threatening to take the pawn, so that White's reply is forced) **3 ♔g4 ♔f7** (the one move which enables him to gain the opposition again, by 4...♔g7, if White comes forward to g5) **4 ♔f4 ♔f6 5 ♔e4 ♔f7! 6 ♔e5 ♔e7** and White is helpless; if he advances the pawn, the only play is similar to that of variation (b): **7 f6+ ♔f7 8 ♔f5** (otherwise the pawn is captured) and we have reached exactly the same position as after move 3 of variation (a).

If the above is not clear, it will quickly become so if you set up the position of Diagram 145 and take each side in turn against a friend, thinking out your moves carefully and each trying to make the most of his chances.

Queening a Lone Pawn

If you are left at the end of a game with a single pawn, every other man on either side (except, of course, the two kings) having been exchanged off, *never move your pawn until you have pushed your king as far forward as possible with safety*. If, in pushing your king forward, you gain the opposition, well and good; you must win unless you make a bad slip. On the other hand, if your opponent gains the opposition, you still have a chance of win-

ning if you can then make a quiet pawn move, for this shifts the burden of the move back to your opponent. You are said to have 'regained the opposition'; now it is he who has to make the retreating king move. If you made one unnecessary pawn move early on, you may have lost the chance of this; for if the pawn is too close to the kings when they clash in opposition, as in variation (a) above, moving it does not help.

That Unqueenable Rook's Pawn

A solitary rook's pawn can never be queened if the defending king can reach the queening square. The attacking king cannot prevent the defender from playing backwards and forwards from the queening square to the next square on the rank. Finally, if the pawn is brought up, we get a position such as that of Diagram 146, where White must either give up his pawn or concede stalemate. If there were another file to the right of the black king, the king would have to move on to it and would lose, as the white king could then move forward and the pawn could be queened; but there is no file to go to, so Black gets a draw by stalemate.

Nor can a rook's pawn queen if the defending king can trap the other in front of it, as in Diagram 147. Black, to play, goes 1 ...

♔c8 and now 2 ♔b6 would allow 2 ... ♔b8 and 3 ... ♔a8 with a draw as in the position on the right, whilst 2 ♔a8 ♔c8 would leave the white king trapped exactly as before.

Diagram 146

Diagram 147

King and Queen *v.* King and Pawn on the Seventh Rank

Earlier we saw how easy it was to give mate with a queen. Even if

Black (as in Diagram 148) has a pawn only one move off its queening square, a white queen can usually prevent its queening, win it and then deliver mate. Exact play is necessary since, if you give Black the least chance, he will queen his pawn and then, with king and queen on each side, nothing but a draw could result except in extraordinary circumstances.

Diagram 148

In Diagram 148 White can win as follows: **1 ♕c4+ ♔b2 2 ♕d3 ♔c1 3 ♕c3+ ♔d1**; now White has a move to spare, as Black cannot queen his pawn without first getting the king out of the way, so: **4 ♔b7! ♔e2 5 ♕c4+ ♔f2 6 ♕d3 ♔e1 7 ♕e3+ ♔d1** and now once again the white king can safely come a square nearer by **8 ♔c6**. When the white king ultimately arrives it is all over.

This winning method fails against a *rook's pawn or a*

bishop's pawn, which provide exceptional cases. Against a pawn on any other file, the queen can win; but see what happens in the case of a rook's pawn (Diagram 149).

Diagram 149

1 ♕a3 ♔b1 2 ♕b3+ ♔a1 and now the black king is stalemated so that if White makes a move with his king he concedes a draw. There is no way of winning.

The case of the bishop's pawn is shown in the next diagram.

Diagram 150

Here **1 ♕b4+ ♔a1 2 ♕c3+ ♔b1 3 ♕b3+ ♔a1!** and if White captures the pawn Black is stalemated.

A Lone Knight Can Stop a Pawn

A solitary knight, when once near enough, can prevent a pawn, supported by a king, from queening. To capture the pawn is the most Black can hope for; a knight alone can never mate, whereas the queen which White would obtain if he were allowed to promote his pawn, could mate Black even against the knight. White cannot in any way advance the pawn without its being captured. This is true even against a pawn on the rook's file, which has the most scope because the knight's movements are impeded by the edge of the board.

Diagram 151

In Diagram 151, White can

drive the knight from the command of a6 by 1 ♔b5 but if, after the reply 1 ... ♘d5, the pawn were to advance the king and pawn would be 'forked' by 2 ... ♘c7+. Wherever White plays his king, the knight can always command the square in front of the pawn, or check, or threaten to fork the king and pawn if the latter advances. This does not apply if a pawn on the rook's file has already reached the seventh rank, for there is no square from which the knight can 'fork' the two squares b7 and a8.

11 Standard Openings

More attention has been devoted to the openings than to any other part of chess. In the course of centuries - literally! - of ceaseless experiment, certain openings have crystallised out as the best and yet - herein lies the eternal attraction of the game - such are the endless possibilities of variation on every move that we are still unable to say that any particular one is *the* best.

For instance, if a player opens with **1 e4**, and his opponent replies likewise with **1 ... e5**, the general consensus of opinion is that the following is the best continuation for both Black and White: **2 ♘f3 ♘c6 3 ♗b5 a6 4 ♗a4 ♘f6 5 0-0 ♗e7 6 ♖e1 b5 7 ♗b3 d6**. This opening is known as the Closed variation of the Ruy Lopez (Spanish) Opening.

On the other hand, after **1 d4**, the following are esteemed to be the best: **1 ... d5 2 c4 e6 3 ♘c3 ♘f6 4 ♗g5 ♗e7 5 e3 ♘bd7 6 ♘f3 0-0 7 ♖c1 c6 8 ♗d3 dxc4 9 ♗xc4 ♘d5 10 ♗xe7 ♕xe7 11 0-0 ♘xc3 12 ♖xc3 e5 13 dxe5 ♘xe5 14 ♘xe5 ♕xe5 15 f4** and so on. This is called the 'Orthodox' variation of the Queen's Gambit Declined. Even though these moves would probably get a good number of votes in a popularity campaign, not one first-class game in a thousand follows them all the way, and many leading masters would vote for others instead. Why is this? Simply because chess holds such infinitely varied possibilities, so many opportunities of divergence.

There are over 72,000 different ways of playing the first four moves alone (two on each side)! This is a magnificent thing. If we were ever able to point to any one particular train of moves and say 'This has been mathematically established as the best,' it would be a bad day for chess - but there is little risk of this ever happening!

The Names of the Openings

The principles of opening play outlined in Chapter 8 will take you along way but, as the openings themselves seem to have a great fascination for learners, and you will soon want to study them more methodically, I shall go into some detail.

Ruy Lopez (or Spanish) Opening: **1 e4 e5 2 ♘f3 ♘c6 3 ♗b5**. Very sound and popular for White at all levels.

Giuoco Piano: **1 e4 e5 2 ♘f3 ♘c6 3 ♗c4**. Sound but stodgy; unfashionable at grandmaster level.

Three or Four Knights Opening: **1 e4 e5 2 ♘f3 ♘c6 3 ♘c3**. Until recently considered very dull but now fashionable due to the English grandmasters Short, Nunn and Chandler.

Scotch Opening: **1 e4 e5 2 ♘f3 ♘c6 3 d4**. White gets his pieces out well but offers little hindrance to Black doing likewise; recently transformed as an attacking weapon by world champion Garry Kasparov.

Petroff's Defence: **1 e4 e5 2 ♘f3 ♘f6**. Previously thought drawish, but now played by many enterprising players.

Greco Counter-Gambit: **1 e4 e5 2 ♘f3 f5**. Lively, but very risky.

Vienna Opening: **1 e4 e5 2 ♘c3**. Complicated, but not often played by grandmasters.

King's Gambit: **1 e4 e5 2 f4**. Doubtful, but exciting; has some brilliant offshoots.

French Defence: **1 e4 e6**. Black is slightly cramped, but will soon launch a counterattack.

Sicilian Defence: **1 e4 c5**. The most lively king's pawn opening; usual choice of Kasparov, former world champion Bobby Fischer and most of the world's leading attacking players.

Caro-Kann Defence: **1 e4 c6**. Fairly sound, but stodgy.

Pirc Defence: **1 e4 d6 2 d4 ♘f6 3 ♘c3 g6**. Counter-attacking fianchetto opening.

Modern Defence: **1 e4 g6 2 d4 ♗g7**. Very similar to Pirc Defence, to which it often transposes.

Centre-Counter Game: **1 e4 d5**. Solid, but not very popular amongst grandmasters.

Alekhine's Defence: **1 e4 ♘f6**. Ingenious, but again not often played at the highest level.

Each of these is characterised by the last move given; thus it is White who decides whether a game shall be a Ruy Lopez or a Giuoco Piano, by moving 3 ♗b5 or 3 ♗c4 as the case may be, but Black who chooses a Sicilian Defence by playing 1 ... c5, or French Defence, by playing 1 ... e6.

Of the above, the Ruy Lopez, French, Caro-Kann and Sicilian are reliable openings, giving excellent prospects to the player who adopts them. The others are perhaps slightly inferior, but the differences are slight and you have to be a strong player to appreciate them properly. Our 'potted comments' give a rough idea of the general character of each opening; they should *not* be taken too seriously. For instance the stodgiest opening may have some brilliant lines of play and an 'unsound' opening may be perfectly good against any but one particular reply.

If the first move is 1 d4. we can have:

Queen's Gambit Declined, Orthodox Defence: **1 d4 d5 2 c4 e6 3 ♘c3 ♘f6**. Sound on both sides.

Queen's Gambit Declined, Tarrasch Defence: **1 d4 d5 2 c4 e6 3 ♘c3 c5**. Ideal for players who like open positions.

Queen's Gambit Declined, Slav Defence: **1 d4 d5 2 c4 c6**. Slightly livelier for Black than the Orthodox.

Queen's Gambit Accepted: **1 d4 d5 2 c4 dxc4**. A little doubtful for Black as he concedes some control of the centre.

Albin Counter Gambit: **1 d4 d5 2 c4 e5**. Interesting, but with accurate play Black should get little for the pawn sacrificed.

Nimzo-Indian Defence: **1 d4 ♘f6 2 c4 e6 3 ♘c3 ♗b4**. Quite possibly the best line for Black, very popular.

Queen's Indian Defence: **1 d4 ♘f6 2 c4 e6 3 ♘f3 b6**. A solid choice; very popular among grandmasters.

King's Indian Defence: **1 d4 ♘f6 2 c4 g6 3 ♘c3 ♗g7**. Considered totally unsound for decades, then became the most popular defence of all. Favoured by players seeking to avoid a draw, as it produces blocked positions which offer scope for manoeuvre.

Grünfeld Defence: **1 d4 ♘f6 2 c4 g6 3 ♘c3 d5**. A complicated but well regarded defence.

Modern Benoni Defence: **1 d4 ♘f6 2 c4 c5 3 d5 e6**. Black is slightly cramped, but has chances of active counterplay.

Benko Gambit: **1 d4 ♘f6 2 c4 c5 3 d5 b5**. Very aggressive, but perhaps not quite sound.

Budapest Gambit: **1 d4 ♘f6 2 c4 e5**. Good for Black only if White tries to keep the gambit pawn.

Dutch Defence: **1 d4 f5**. A counter-attack, intending sharp kingside play; development of Black's queenside tends to lag.

Of these, the soundest are undoubtedly: the Queen's Gambit Declined, Orthodox Defence; the Queen's Gambit Declined, Slav Defence; the Nimzo-Indian Defence; the Queen's Indian Defence; the King's Indian Defence; and the Grünfeld Defence. The Albin Counter-Gambit is the most unsound (for the player who makes the characteristic move, of course).

There are other quite sound alternative first moves for White, e.g.

English Opening: **1 c4**. Often played by Kasparov and former world champion Anatoly Karpov, and

Réti Opening: **1 ♘f3**. A somewhat vague opening (c2-c4, d2-d4 or e2-e4 is usually played afterwards, so the same positions are often reached as when the pawn move preceded the knight move).

There is also the none too sound but lively

Bird's Opening: **1 f4** and its even livelier offshoot

From's Gambit: **1 f4 e5** which would better be named 'From's Counter-Gambit' as we usually call it a *counter-gambit* when it is Black who sacrifices.

So we have outlined some of the most popular openings - but there are still many off-shoots of these openings to be catalogued. Although it would obviously be outside the scope of this little book to examine any in detail, we shall briefly describe a few popular ones, taken at random.

The King's Gambit
(1 e4 e5 2 f4)

Black does best to accept the gambit by 2 ... exf4. Now White typically goes all out for quick development, usually playing ♘f3, ♗c4, 0-0, at full speed, then d4 and capturing the gambit pawn on f4 with his queen's bishop. His queen goes to e2 or f3 and his queen's rook usually to e1. The basic idea of the opening is an attack on the pawn on f7 by White's king's bishop on c4 and his king's rook, or his king's rook and queen in collaboration along the open f-file.

Black has a choice of two contrasting systems of defence. He can try to protect the gambit pawn by ... g7-g5 in which case

White often challenges the protecting pawn by h2-h4; or he can play ... d7-d5, counter-sacrificing this pawn, if necessary, and securing a fine, mobile development of all his pieces.

The Sicilian Defence
(1 e4 c5)

If White omits to play d2-d4, the game takes on a slow, rather solid character, which need not trouble Black much. But if White plays d2-d4, Black captures with his c-pawn and now has an open c-file which he should exploit as energetically as possible, by placing his queen's rook and queen on it, manoeuvring a knight to c4 and so on. His king's bishop is often well developed on g7 (after ... g7-g6); his other bishop can go either to b7 or to e6, his king's knight to f6, his king's rook (after 0-0) to d8.

Diagram 152

Black should play ... d7-d5 when he can do so safely. Diagram 152 shows a typical development for him - and a satisfactory one - in the case, which frequently occurs, when he can not.

White usually strives for c2-c4; if he can play this safely soon, the pawn can usually be held there and cramps Black's efforts on the c-file, gripping him in what is known as the 'Maroczy Bind' (named after the Hungarian master who discovered its power). White castles on the kingside like Black and attacks in the centre and on the king's wing, the move f2-f4-f5 forming a typical climax to his preparations.

The Queen's Gambit (1 d4 d5 2 c4)

The Queen's Gambit Accepted has the disadvantage (for Black) of permitting White to get in e2-e4 as well as d2-d4, almost without hindrance (though White best precedes e2-e4 by 3 ♘f3 to prevent 3 ... e5, a counter-sacrifice as effective as Black's ... d5 in the King's Gambit mentioned above). In the Gambit Declined, Black's early ... e6 rather obstructs the development of his queen's bishop; the alternative ... c6 of the Slav Defence leaves the way clear for Black's queen's bishop but is not significantly superior.

Why Black Cannot Keep the Queen's Gambit Pawn

To call this opening a 'gambit' is not strictly correct, for any attempt by Black to retain the gambit pawn meets with disaster, thus (after 1 d4 d5 2 c4 dxc4)

3　♘f3　　b5
4　e3

Better than 4 e4 for the special purposes of punishing Black's wrong methods.

4　...　　c6

The best way of preparing against White's next.

5　a4　　♕b6

5 ... bxa4 would leave all four of Black's queenside pawns pitifully isolated and weak.

6　axb5　　cxb5

6 ... ♕xb5 would isolate the c-pawn, leaving it weak, and expose the queen to attack.

7　♘e5

Diagram 153

7　...　　♘f6

Directed against the possibility of 8 ♕f3 which would simultaneously threaten 9 ♕xa8 and 9 ♕xf7+. 7 ... ♘f6 develops a piece and screens the f-pawn. If 7 ... ♗b7 to screen the rook instead, White proceeds 8 b3 cxb3 9 ♕xb3 as in the game.

8 b3 cxb3

Obviously forced, for this pawn was attacked three times over and even were it given extra protection now (e.g. by 8 ... ♗e6) it would only be protected twice.

9 ♕xb3

Diagram 154

Threatening 10 ♗xb5+ and 10 ♕xf7+; Black cannot prevent both of these so must return the pawn. He has therefore loosened his position for no good reason.

The Nimzo-Indian Defence
(1 d4 ♘f6 2 c4 e6 3 ♘c3 ♗b4)

The main idea of this defence is to interfere seriously with White's playing e2-e4. By 3 ... ♗b4, pinning White's queen's knight, Black renders illusory the knight's guard over e4 - do you remember our remarks about the pinned knight in Diagram 84? - so that 4 e4? would be answered by 4 ... ♘xe4, simply and safely. Black often follows up with ... b7-b6 and ... ♗b7, to get a further purchase on White's e4-square. He must be prepared to exchange his king's bishop for the knight it is pinning, experience having shown that the effect (in the centre) of this exchange justifies his parting with one of his bishops.

Traps

In every opening there exist a few extraordinary 'traps', whereby certain moves receive drastic punishment. As a rule, it is a slightly bad move which is punishable in this way, but occasionally a move which nobody could criticise on general grounds can be ruthlessly exploited by a series of forced moves. As an example, take the 'Noah's Ark' trap, so called (I believe) on account of its antiquity.

This occurs in the well-known opening known as the Ruy Lopez, after a great Spanish player of that name who lived in the fifteenth century. We have already given one variation of the Ruy Lopez. We now diverge at White's fifth move.

1	e4	e5
2	♘f3	♘c6
3	♗b5	a6
4	♗a4	♘f6
5	♘c3	d6
6	d4	b5
7	♗b3	

This seems a very natural move here, but as a consequence of the trap we are going to show, White would be better advised to play 7 dxe5 instead, countering Black's threat to his bishop with a threat to Black's knight.

7	...	exd4
8	♘xd4	

Otherwise he just loses a pawn.

8	...	♘xd4
9	♕xd4	

Things do not look too bad.

9	...	c5

Diagram 155

But now White's queen is attacked; wherever he retreats it, Black continues with 10 ... c4 next move and the bishop now attacked has no escape, and is lost.

To avoid disaster through traps, firstly, cultivate a sound style of play. This will come naturally to you if you have assimilated the advice in Chapters 6, 7 and 8, and you will be preserved from the majority of traps. Secondly, when you become restless and want to rise above Diagram 131 and its accompanying maxims, study books on chess openings; learn by heart whatever few stock traps exist in the particular openings you adopt.

The Psychological Factor

Between the best 'line' in an opening and scores of variations arising from it there may be only the slightest difference. Because your opponent is a human being, condemned to find a good reply to each of your move within a limited time, an inferior move which catches him unawares may trouble him more than a perfectly good move he is prepared for.

Other factors come in. Individual style is of much account in chess. You can pick up a game-score you have never seen before, play it over and say 'I think that is one of Alekhine's games' just as you could identify an unknown piece of music as Debussy's. One player will always feel happier with pieces slung about the board in a wild attack; another, who prefers solid, quiet play, will feel profoundly uncomfortable in just such a position, even though his attacking chances might be sufficiently good to give him the better prospects. An opening which is good against the first may be bad against the second. If your opponent is ill-at-ease because of the whole 'feel' of a position, it is little consolation to him to know vaguely that somewhere in some book whose name he cannot recall even were he allowed to leave the board to consult it, some master has demonstrated that, after the precise move you have just played, it is possible to gain a definite advantage by just one particular train of six or seven select moves. Even the masters are far from omniscient on the openings - they are only human (a fact which occasionally seems to cause surprise). The famous master Tarrasch once 'caught out' an opponent in the opening with a variation he had previously analysed privately for weeks, winning a piece and the game. The game won great publicity and 'Tarrasch's Trap' became famous overnight. In spite of this, a few years later another master fell headlong into the same trap and lost a piece in the exact same way. No master knows every opening, some know surprisingly few. Others are walking encyclopaedias on the subject, but have lost, as well as gained, through concentrating so exhaustively on one particular part of the game.

12 Problems and Practical Pay

Chess Problems

Chess problems form a branch of the game so distinct that keen problemists may not play a proper game for years. Most chess addicts, however, intersperse problem-solving with game play, and get all the more out of chess thereby. On the whole, problems receive more support from the newspaper chess columnists, chess play more from the clubs.

A chess problem consists of a diagrammed position in which, by starting with one particular move, White can checkmate his opponent within a stipulated number of moves, in the face of whatever defence the latter may put up. That one initial move is the 'solution' or 'key-move' or 'key' to the problem. No other move will do.

The art of chess problems consists in making this key the very last move you would expect, or introducing beautiful or subtle play, Black making clever attempts at defence which White brilliantly frustrates. Here is a very simple problem: White to play and mate in two moves.

Diagram 156

Note, by the way, that in problems White is almost always regarded as playing *up* the board.

The key is 1 ♖c2; there follows 1 ... bxc2 2 b4 mate. You would not expect that the only way for White to force mate in two moves is to allow Black to capture his best piece. But it is so. Other moves by the rook would all leave Black stalemated; moves by the white king or bishop would either allow the black king to attain freedom in the upper part of the board or, even if they were to keep him more or less confined towards the lower part, never render it possible to mate him next move. For instance: 1 ♗d3 ♔a4 2 ♖h4+ ♔a5, etc. or 1 ♔c6 ♔b4 2 ♖h4+ ♔a5. In this latter 'variation', White can now mate by 3 ♖a4, but as he has taken three moves instead of the stipulated two, he has *not* solved the problem.

A Complex Three-Move Problem

Space being restricted, I cannot go into problems at length but will pass on at once to a typically complex 'three-mover'. Diagram 157 is no ordinary problem but one of the finest ever composed.

White has to play and mate Black in three moves.

Examining the position as if it had been reached in an ordinary game, we see that Black is threatening to queen his pawn next move. On the other hand, his king is in a corner, where any piece is at a disadvantage, and may receive a discovered check from the bishop at any moment through the knight, which now screens it from the bishop, moving away. Two pieces, such as this knight and bishop, which are posted ready to deliver a discovered check, are said to form a 'battery'.

Composed by C. S. Kipping.

Diagram 157

From these flimsy advantages, White can build up a brilliant forced mate.

Suppose we capture the pawn when it queens: 1 ♘d4+ ♔a7 2 ♘f3 ♔xa6 ... what now? Or 1 ♘d4+ ♔a7 2 ♘c2 ♖g1 and Black is threatening to recapture the knight which captures his promoted pawn.

In neither of these cases, and in no way by interfering with the queening of the pawn, can White hope to win the game at all, let alone mate Black within a few moves. Nor is it any use discovering the bishop check on the first move in any other way. Trial confirms these statements. We might try all sorts of other moves by the bishop or knights and find them all wanting. For instance 1 ♗xg2 e1(♕) gets nowhere - White might actually lose.

What of a move by the white king, such as 1 ♔b5. This threat-

ens 2 ♔b6, after which Black is
threatened by mate in no fewer
than nine different ways, namely
by 3 ♘c7, or by any one of the
eight different possible moves of
the other knight which discover
check from the bishop.

We should have to be very
wide-awake to discover the one
drawback to 1 ♔b5 as a key-
move: the reply 1 ... ♖g8. Now, if
2 ♔b6 ♖c8! interfering with
every one of the nine threatened
mates for, if 3 ♘c7+ ♖xc7; and if
the other knight moves to discover check, the rook can interpose, postponing the mate for one
move (here is an essential difference between play and problems;
a player would say 'What is the
difference? I mate next move, in
any case,' whereas a problemist
would reply 'It is a mate in three
moves, *not* in four, and there is
all the difference in the world.'
Nor would any other second
move by White, after 1 ... ♖g8,
avail, so 1 ♔b5 cannot be the
key-move.

It is **1 ♔a5!!** - apparently the
most suicidal move on the board -
allowing Black to queen his pawn
with check. Now, after 1 ...
e1(♕)+ White must not be nervous and reply with 2 ♘b4+ for
there would then be no mate after
2 ... ♔a7. He must calmly proceed 2 ♔b6, inviting four more
different checks from the black
queen and one from the rook,
everything is neat and harmoni-
ous.

We will find to our delight that
the welter of threats we mentioned when considering 1 ♔b5
as a possible key move is now
sufficient to cope with anything
the new-born queen can achieve.
Thus (assuming the moves 1 ♔a5
e1(♕)+ 2 ♔b6 have been made),
whether the new queen checks
along a file or a diagonal, White
can interpose the knight discovering check (and mate). Such brilliant counterstrokes are rare in
games. One of the positions
which might result is shown in
the next diagram.

Diagram 158

Going back to the original
position of Diagram 157, of
course Black, in reply to the key
move 1 ♔a5, need not promote
the pawn. We found that 1 ... ♖g8
saved him after 1 ♔b5. Does it
now? No! 1 ♔a5 ♖g8 2 ♘d4+
♔a7 3 ♘b5 mate. We could not
give this mate before, because the
white king stood on the square to
which the knight finally wanted

to go.

The beauty of the problem is clear. White makes two apparently suicidal moves in succession. Only thus can he give mate on the third; if he adopts any of the numerous apparently safer alternatives offered him he loses all chance of attaining his goal.

The 'try' or 'nearly-a-solution' by 1 ♗b5 is particularly attractive, and even experienced solvers might assume that this is the key-move, overlooking the fact that Black, by one super-subtle resource, can postpone mate by an all-important move.

Don't tackle any 'mate in three' problem until you have solved forty or fifty 'mate in two'. You will only break your heart; a good three-mover may take even an expert two hours to solve. In the three-mover we have just dealt with, there were many other alternative possibilities we have not touched on. You can learn a lot by working these out at leisure, or doing the same with other problems, of which you know the key-moves.

Do this with Diagrams 175 and 176 later on. Don't be ashamed of looking up the key-move if you fail to solve one within half an hour or so but don't be too lazy to give it a thorough examination after that. Remember that there is an adequate reply to *every* move Black can make in answer to the key-move. Also, take it from me that no other first move by White,

apart from the given key-move, will solve the problem. A second solution, or 'cook' as it is called, is regarded as a serious blemish, rendering the problem worthless.

Waiting Problems

The next diagram shows an interesting type of problem called a 'waiting problem' or 'waiter'.

Composed by J A W Hunter in 1872.

Diagram 159

Suppose, for a moment, that it were Black's turn to play instead of White's; we will find on examination that whatever move he were to make, White could mate him in reply, e.g.

If 1 ... ♗ moves 2 ♖d4 mate.
If 1 ... c3+ 2 ♕xd3 mate.
If 1 ... ♖e2 2 ♖xe2 mate (the black bishop being pinned).
If 1 ... ♖e3 2 ♘c3 mate.

If 1 ... ♖f3 2 ♗f5 mate.
If 1 ... ♖(f1)-anywhere else 2 ♘f2 mate.
If 1 ... f3 2 ♗f5 mate.
If 1 ... h5 2 ♘xg5 mate.
If 1 ♘ anywhere 2 ♖e7 mate.
If 1 ... d4 2 ♕b7 mate.

These ready-made mating variations are called 'set mates'.

No more moves for Black are possible and so apparently all White needs to do is to find some *waiting move* which leaves the situation essentially unaltered. What about 1 ♕c2. No, there would then be no mate after 1 ... d4. Similarly 1 ♖f8 fails to provide for 1 ... ♘e7 and 1 ♗a1 or 1 ♗c3 for 1 ... d4.

The move which solves the conundrum and consequently the key-move of the problem, is 1 ♗h8!. At first glance it might seem extraordinary that this bashful-looking retirement into the corner, *which threatens nothing*, achieves something which none of the many violent alternatives can - encompass Black's downfall in two moves. This is an excellent example of the artificiality - and beauty - of chess problems.

Sometimes in a problem, every Black move in the original position will have been provided for as above, but there is no perfect waiting move by White; then the key-move will abandon one or more of the original mating combinations, replacing them usually by more spectacular ones.

This is even a more beautiful type of problem, called a 'mutate'.

Or 'set mates' can be altered by the key-move in a problem which is not a 'waiter' at all - they all called 'changed mates' and the problem a 'change-mate'.

Zugzwang

Though to have the move in chess is, nine hundred and ninety-nine times out of a thousand, an advantage, exceptional positions exist where it is a liability and even, as we have seen when considering diagrams 141 and 145, a fatal liability. A player who is in the unfortunate situation of having to accelerate his own downfall by making a move is said to be 'move-bound' or 'in Zugzwang' (a German word meaning 'move-compulsion'). 'Under duress' is another good term. The next diagram shows a classic instance of this state of affairs which occurred in a master game in 1923. Black now went 1 ... h6!, leaving White move-bound.

White's queen has several possible moves now, but all are obviously suicidal. Let us examine White's other possible moves, one by one; we shall see that he can only bring about his own downfall:

2 ♘c3 or 2 ♘a3; 2 ... bxc3 or 2 ... bxa3 wins a piece.
2 ♗c3 bxc3 wins a piece.
2 ♗c1 ♗xb1 wins a piece.

2 ♖e1-anywhere, 2 ... ♖e2 wins the queen.

2 ♖gf1 ♗xf1 wins a piece in the end.

2 ♔h2 ♖5f3 which, since White's king's bishop is now pinned, wins the queen.

2 ♗f1 ♖5f3 wins the queen.

2 g4 ♖5f3 and wins the queen, since 2 ♗xf3 would allow mate by 2 ... ♖h2.

2 h4 ♖5f3 3 ♗xf3 ♖xf3; Black wins queen and bishop for two rooks, since the attacked queen has now no escape.

2 ♗xb4 ♗xb4 wins a piece.

Diagram 160

The lesson of these positions is - have a mental look at every position *from your opponent's point of view*. He may be suffering from difficulties of which, but for this survey, you would not become aware. In this, as in many other ways, chess is a marvellous training for the problems of our daily life.

How many frightful blunders, of international magnitude, could have been avoided in the past, *if only somebody had put himself in the other man's position.*

A Typical Sacrificial Attack against the Castled King

In this book, I have dealt mainly with simple principles involving a few pieces at a time, because they are the easiest to understand and the principles involved in the most complicated position are often compounded of very simple elements. But I should disappoint, were I not to give at least one example of the beautiful possibilities that arise through the co-ordination of several pieces.

Diagram 161

Here is a rather more complicated type of thing - an attack which can easily develop out of the opening and which introduces a bishop-sacrifice playable surprisingly often when Black's king's knight has been driven away from its ideal position at f6 (by the advance of White's king's pawn to e5, for instance). White plays:

1 &xh7+! &xh7
2 ♕h5+ &g8
3 ♘g5

Threatening to mate by 4 ♕h7. Neither 3 ... g6 nor 3 ... f6 would prevent this, in fact the only moves to postpone it are 3 ... ♕xg5 (which gives away a queen for a knight, as the queen can be recaptured) and 3 ... ♖e8 or 3 ... ♖d8, which only postpone the mate for one move, e.g. 4 ♕h7+ &f8 5 ♕h8 mate.

Thus White's sacrifice of a bishop on his first move is well repaid. If Black were to decline to take the bishop, playing 1 ... &h8 instead, White could proceed 2 ♕h5 just the same, and now the threat is to deliver a discovered check from the queen by 3 &g6 and mate by 4 ♕h7. Against this Black can do nothing.

Diagram 162

A similar sacrifice is often playable when White's queen and queen's bishop are still on their original squares as in Diagram 162. White plays 1 &xh7+ and Black replies with 1 ... &xh7 as before; in this case, 2 ♘g5+ comes before ♕h5 and if Black answers the knight check by 2 ... &g6 instead of 2 ... &g8 3 ♕g4 is now almost as powerful as was ♕h5 in the line given above (if then 3 ... f5 4 ♕h4!).

Winning Practice

To conclude, I give a few positions in each of which White can achieve something effective. In each case, principles utilised in doing so are disclosed, in brackets or otherwise. Every example holds some hidden twist. If you can solve half of them, you can congratulate yourself on having already gained a better grasp of chess than the individual who has been playing for a year, without bothering to read a book about it.

Solutions are on pages 134-137.

Obviously the win for White in Diagram 163 is only a matter of time. You are not asked to go into the quite involved play which may precede the inevitable end but merely to state which is the best first move by White, i.e. the one which will enable him to mate Black the quickest ... and why? (*Queen's 'barrier' across* board.)

Diagram 163

The position in the next diagram can arise very naturally from a Queen's Gambit opening, thus: 1 d4 d5 2 c4 e6 3 ♘c3 ♘f6 4 ♗g5 ♘bd7 5 cxd5 exd5.

Diagram 164

This could be regarded as a trap in the opening. White might feel tempted to play 6 ♘xd5, as the knight on Black's f6, which apparently protects the pawn, is pinned against his queen. *Would*

White be wise to play 6 ♘xd5...?

Diagram 165

By a brilliant queen sacrifice, White can finish the game in three moves. How? (*Double check.*)

Diagram 166

An important pendant to the notes on rook and pawn endgames on pages 88-90. It illustrates two special dangers to the defending side where he has managed to compensate for being a pawn down by getting his rook into the ideal position, *behind* the passed pawn. Black's pawn is one square off queening. White can draw, but by *one move* only. What is that move, and why? (*Skewer*.)

Diagram 167

Diagram 167 shows a common case of a careless pin. Black has just played ... ♗g4 thinking that this immobilises White's king's knight. But it actually allows White to win a pawn. How? (*'Manufactured' fork.*)

Diagram 168

On page 115 we gave the first 7 moves of the Ruy Lopez. After three moves on each side, in the following position, it looks as if White could win a pawn by 4 ♗xc6 (destroying the protection of Black's e-pawn) followed by 5 ♘xe5. But Black has two different ways of recovering the pawn, one using a fork and the other a half-pin, and employing the same piece for the job each time. What are they?

The next example is rather neat. Black, to move, can win White's queen in two moves on each side, making use first of a discovered attack and then of an over-burdened man; the fact that the white queen is unprotected also plays its part.

Diagram 169

The next is also rather neat. It exploits an overburdened man, a discovered attack and an unprotected piece. White to move and win at least a piece.

Diagram 170

The next is a quaint example of two black men being equally over-burdened with the same duty - that of preventing mate on the back rank of the type shown in Diagram 32. White to move and win a pawn at once.

Diagram 171

In the next example, Black can win by a brilliant series of checks. He employs a double check, a fork and a skewer.

Diagram 172

White's pawn is twice attacked (by rook and knight) but only once defended (by bishop). Can he therefore safely capture it with his knight? (*Pin, fork.*)

Diagram 173

A simple position, which conceals extraordinary combinative possibilities. White, to play, can within three moves force and endgame in which the clear advantage of two pawns ensures victory. Remember that a pawn reaching the eighth rank need not necessarily become a *queen*. (*'Manufactured' fork.*)

Diagram 174

Finally, two problems by the author.
Composed by B. H. Wood.

Diagram 175

White to play and mate on his second move against any defence.

Composed by B. H. Wood.

Diagram 176

White to play and mate in three moves against any defence.

Conclusion

If you take chess very seriously, you may derive a lifetime of enjoyment from the study of it. On the other hand, the general principles I have outlined, with plenty of practice, could make you a strong player without studying any other book on chess at all.

Do not underestimate Diagram 131. Learn it by heart. Followed intelligently, the system based on it would give you not the very best, but a satisfactory opening against the strongest player in the world. What more could you ask for than a system which enables you to emerge from the opening stages with a perfectly satisfactory game - and a system readily understood and, indeed, expoundable in its broad outlines within a few paragraphs? This is what I have given you.

In bringing out your forces 'never move any piece until you have moved every piece once' is an excellent general maxim (I said general!).

On the other hand, you will of course benefit from a close study of the exact opening lines given earlier in the previous chapter.

At all times, be on the alert to take advantage of blunders by your opponent, also to exploit incidental weaknesses by forks, pins, skewers, discovered attacks, etc. In the many positions which offer no such clean-cut chances, and which could otherwise be puzzling to you, you can estimate the value of potential moves by Weaver Adams' method which ensures that you consistently improve the general disposition of your men and stand, therefore, ever prepared for any sudden chance the game may offer. Does moving this man give it extra power or mobility, or rob enemy men of power or mobility? Does it create weaknesses in the enemy camp or does it remove one of your own? Does it produce a passed pawn? Or over-burden some man? Or leave two pieces prone to a fork? Or start a 'pawn roller'? Soon these questions should become habitual.

Though I wish I could have spared space for more examples illustrating the various principles, every game you play will provide scores of such examples and illustrations, if you only keep your eyes open for them. Advice you do not understand now may come back to you in a blinding light some day when you suddenly realise how easily you can win a game with its aid.

You are only on the threshold of the delights of chess. Play plenty of games, re-read this little book occasionally - every time you do so it should convey a little more - treat your games seriously and you will soon begin to develop a new mental power. Some jobs in life, once mastered, never really test your intelligence again, but chess in your leisure time can brush away the cobwebs, give you a new alertness, keep you up to scratch mentally and develop in you, year after year, a keener, brighter outlook on life.

It is game to revel in when you are 'on top of the world'; it is a game to provide inestimable solace when you feel rebuffed and dispirited.

Solutions

Diagram 163
1 ♕f5

On this square, by means of the 'barriers' it sets up along a rank and a file, the queen at once confines the black king to four squares in the centre of the board, so that White can bring up his king confident in the knowledge that the black king cannot run away.

Diagram 164
No! 6 ♘xd5 would lose a piece: Black can reply 6 ... ♘xd5! for if 7 ♗xd8 then 7 ... ♗b4+ 8 ♕d2 (*the only legal move!*) 8 ... ♗xd2+ 9 ♔xd2 ♔xd8 ...

Diagram 165
1   ♕d8+   ♔xd8
No choice!
2   ♗g5+
and now, on 2 ... ♔e8 3 ♖d8 is mate. On 2 ... ♔c7 3 ♗d8 is mate.

Diagram 166
Black is threatening 1 ... ♖c1+ 2 ♔ moves h1(♕) and now the black rook and queen protect each other. So the white king must go to the second rank, in order to capture the black rook if the latter checks. After 1 ♔c2 or 1 ♔d2 Black could play 1 ... ♖a1 2 ♖xh2 ♖a2+ and win the white rook by a skewer. Hence White must play 1 ♔b2, leave the king there and then, as explained after Diagram 110, Black is helpless.

Diagram 167
I said that a piece pinned against a queen is immobilised *unless it has brilliant work to do*. Here White's king's knight has brilliant work to do: 1 ♗xf7+ ♔xf7 (otherwise Black loses a pawn without a fight) 2 ♘e5+ (setting

up the fork 'manufactured' by 1 ♗xf7+) 2 ... ♔ moves 3 ♘xg4 ♘xg4 4 ♕xg4 and White has won a pawn.
1 ♘e5 at once is playable and good (if 1 ... ♗xd1? 2 ♗xf7 mate) but Black can play 1 ... ♗e6 2 ♗xe6 fxe6 and, though Black's kingside pawns have been broken up, he has not actually lost a pawn.

Diagram 168
Black recaptures with the d-pawn (4 ♗xc6) 4 ... dxc6 5 ♘xe5 and now plays 5 ... ♕d4! forking the white king's knight and king pawn and capturing one of them next move.
Or he recaptures with the b-pawn (4 ♗xc6) 4 ... bxc6 5 ♘xe5 and sets up a half-pin of the white knight and e-pawn against his king by 5 ... ♕e7. If White now moves the knight, Black plays 6 ... ♕xe4+. If White protects the knight it must first be driven away by 6 ... d6.

Diagram 169
Black plays 1 ... ♖xg3+. This has uncovered an attack by Black's queen onto White's, so White has no time for 2 hxg3 or 2 ♗xg3. He can play 2 ♔f1 protecting the queen but now Black sets up a murderous pin by 2 ... ♗b5 (he could also win the queen for the rook by 2 ... ♖g1+).

Diagram 170
White simply plays 1 ♘xe6 and if

Black is so injudicious as to re-capture (1 ... fxe6) he loses his queen by 2 ♗g6+ hxg6 (or 2 ... ♔ moves) 3 ♕xa3. Black's f-pawn is over-burdened with the double task of protecting the bishop and preventing ♗g6+ by White, with its discovered attack on the un-supported black queen.

Diagram 171
White plays 1 ♖xb7 and, al-though both White's rooks are unsupported, neither of the black rooks can capture or the other will be captured with mate on the back rank. The fact that one of a piece's duties is to prevent a mate on the back rank can easily be overlooked.

Diagram 172
1 ... ♖f1+ 2 ♔xf1 (as it is a *dou-ble* check, the king must move, e.g. 2 ♖xc5 would still leave him in check) 2 ... ♘g3+ 3 ♔e1 ♕e3+ 4 ♔d1 ♕e2+ 5 ♔c1 ♕e1+ 6 ♔c2 ♕xe4+ 7 ♔c1 (any other move would allow Black to take the queen for nothing) 7 ... ♘e2+ (and now the queen goes anyway) 8 ♔d1 ♕xb1+ 9 ♔xe2 ♕xb2+ and Black should win easily.

Diagram 173
Yes, White can then pin the knight against the black rook by ♖e1 but this apparently powerful move fails against Black's re-source (first play the moves 1 ... ♘xe5 2 ♖e1) 2 ... ♘g6! so that if White now takes the rook 3

♖xe6? Black regains the rook and the bishop aswell, by 3 ... ♘xf4+ 4 ♔ moves ♘xe6.

Diagram 174
1　♖c8+　♖xc8
If 1 ... ♔xb7 2 ♖xd8.
2　♕xa7+　♔xa7
3　bxc8(♘)+
becoming a knight, giving check and then 4 ♘xe7.

Diagram 175
1 d6
If 1 ... cxd6 2 ♕e4.
1 ... ♔d4 2 ♕c3.
1 ... ♔e6 2 ♕d5.
1 ... ♔f5 or 1 ... ♔f4 2 ♕e4.

Diagram 176
1 ♘e3
Threatening 2 ♖g4+ ♔e5 3 ♖e4 mate.
If 1 ... ♘f2 or 1 ... ♘e5+ 2 ♔e6 (a waiting move; nothing is threatened but Black cannot move without letting in a mate).
If 1 ... ♘e5 2 ♖g4 (threat 3 ♖e4 mate; if 2 ... ♘f2 or 2 ... ♘f4 to prevent this, 3 d4 mate).
Weaknesses of this problem lie in the necessity to provide against the threatened check to the white king, also in the dual continua-tions after 1 ... f2 or 1 ... ♘(b4) moves, each of which, however, lead to neat mates.
After 1 ... f2, either 2 ♘g2+ ♔e5 3 ♖g5 mate, or 2 ♖g4+ ♔f3 3 ♘d4 mate.
After 1 ... ♘(b4) moves, either 2 ♖g4+ and 3 ♖e4 mate or 2

♘d5+ and 3 ♖g5 mate.

Attractive features of the problem are the good key (giving the black king a flight square) and the quiet second moves such as 2 ♔e6 or 2 ♖g4.

Appendix

The World Championship

Through the centuries, a number of players were generally acknowledged as the world's best, e.g. Ruy Lopez (Spain), about 1575, Philidor (France) about 1750, followed by his countrymen Deschapelles and de La Bourdonnais, then England's Staunton, Morphy from America, and Anderssen from Germany, but Steinitz was the first to be recognised as 'World Champion'. Since then there have been numerous matches for the title: (in each case the eventual winner's name is given first)

1886	**Steinitz**-Zukertort	12½-7½	New York, St Louis, and New Orleans
1889	**Steinitz**-Tchigorin	10½-6½	Havana
1890/1	**Steinitz**-Gunsberg	10½-8½	New York
1892	**Steinitz**-Tchigorin	12½-10½	Havana
1894	**Lasker**-Steinitz	12-7	New York, Philadelphia and Montreal
1896/7	**Lasker**-Steinitz	12½-4½	Moscow
1907	**Lasker**-Marshall	11½-3½	USA
1908	**Lasker**-Tarrasch	10½-5½	Dusseldorf and Munich
1910	**Lasker**-Schlechter	5-5	Vienna and Berlin
1910	**Lasker**-Janowski	9½-1½	Berlin
1921	**Capablanca**-Lasker	9-5	Havana
1927	**Alekhine**-Capablanca	18½-15½	Buenos Aires
1929	**Alekhine**-Bogolyubov	15½-9½	Germany and Holland
1934	**Alekhine**-Bogolyubov	15½-10½	Germany
1935	**Euwe**-Alekhine	15½-14½	Holland
1937	**Alekhine**-Euwe	15½-9½	Holland
	(Alekhine died, March 1946)		
1948	(FIDE Tournament, The Hague, Moscow: **Botvinnik** 14, Smyslov 11, Keres and Reshevsky 10½, Euwe 4)		
1951	**Botvinnik**-Bronstein	12-12	Moscow

1954	**Botvinnik**-Smyslov	12-12	Moscow
1957	**Smyslov**-Botvinnik	12½-9½	Moscow
1958	**Botvinnik**-Smyslov	12½-10½	Moscow
1960	**Tal**-Botvinnik	12½-8½	Moscow
1961	**Botvinnik**-Tal	13-8	Moscow
1963	**Petrosian**-Botvinnik	12½-9½	Moscow
1966	**Petrosian**-Spassky	12½-11½	Moscow
1969	**Spassky**-Petrosian	12½-10½	Moscow
1972	**Fischer**-Spassky	12½-8½	Reykjavik
1975	(Karpov became champion, after Fischer refused to defend his title)		
1978	**Karpov**-Korchnoi	16½-15½	Baguio
1981	**Karpov**-Korchnoi	11-7	Merano
1984/5	Karpov-Kasparov	25-23	Moscow (match abandoned without decision)
1985	**Kasparov**-Karpov	13-11	Moscow
1986	**Kasparov**-Karpov	12½-11½	London/Leningrad
1987	**Kasparov**-Karpov	12-12	Seville
1990	**Kasparov**-Karpov	12½-11½	NewYork/Lyons
	(Kasparov and Short broke from FIDE in 1993 to form the PCA; Karpov and Timman contested the vacant FIDE title)		
1993	**Kasparov**-Short	12½-7½	London (PCA)
1993	**Karpov**-Timman	12½-8½	Zwolle, Arnhem, Amsterdam, Jakarta (FIDE)

Index and Glossary

Here is an alphabetical list of chess terms used in this book, together with others you may encounter. Figures refer to pages where the term in question is defined or elaborated. I have omitted some terms as self-evident or abstruse. The original version of this glossary was the first ABC of chess on this scale ever attempted.

For definition of names of squares, ranks, files, moves, pieces, etc., such as 'queen's bishop', 'g-pawn', 'king's knight', 'a-pawn', 'e-file', 'e4' etc., see Chapter 9.

Terms in italics are peculiar to problems.

Active Chess: See Rapid Chess.
Adjournment: p 54.
Adjudication: Examination by a strong player of the position reached in a game which cannot be finished, to decide how the game would probably have terminated.
Adjust: Correct the positioning of a piece on its square.
Advanced pawn: Pawn on its fifth rank or beyond.
Advantage: To hold the better position.

Alapin Opening: 1 e4 e5 2 ♘e2. Rotten!
Albin Counter-gambit: p 117.
Alekhine's Defence: p 116.
Algebraic notation: The international standard system of notation explained in Chapter 9. The board is regarded exclusively from White's side; the files, from left to right, are lettered 'a' to 'h' and the ranks from bottom to top are numbered 1 to 8. The fact that each square has only one name aids in discussion; thus instead of 'White's K6' or 'Black's K3' we say simply 'e6'.
All-play-all: Tournament for individuals in which each plays every other once, or occasionally twice or four times.
American tournament: Same as 'all-play-all'.
Analysis (of a position): Search for the best subsequent moves by each side.
Annotation: Commentary on a game.
Antiquity of Chess: The earliest authenticated references to chess occur in Persian manuscripts about 600AD. Relics of games played by men with differentiated functions on a chequered board

have been found in Egyptian tombs, 3,000 years old. The greatest developments of the game have been successively in India, about 600AD, then Persia, Arabia, Spain, Italy, Western Europe. Today the leading chess country is Russia.

Any?: Abbreviation in Kriegspiel for 'Can I make any pawn captures?'

Arbiter: Supervisor who ensures that the rules of chess are obeyed.

Artificially isolated pawn: A pawn supportable only by another pawn which, being badly blocked by a hostile man, is unlikely to ever be able to come to its aid.

Attack: (a) To threaten to take; (b) An offensive action in one part of the board.

Automaton (chessplaying): A spoof 'mechanical' chessplayer, which caused a sensation more than once when exhibited in the nineteenth century. The 'body' of the monster concealed a diminutive expert who operated the hands which made the moves with the help of a system of magnets.

Back rank (A player's): The rank on which his pieces start the game.

Back-rank mate: Checkmate by a queen or rook on the last rank.

Backward pawn: p 81.

Bad bishop: p 91.

Barrier (set up by rook or queen): p 28.

Battery: p 124.

BCF: (The) British Chess Federation. The official British governing body. Readers wishing to contact the BCF should write to BCF, 9a Grand Parade, St Leonards-on-Sea, East Sussex TN38 0DD.

BCM: British Chess Magazine, a monthly founded in 1881. For further details write to BCM, 69 Masbro Road, London W14 0LS.

BCPS: British Chess Problem Society.

Beauty prize: Prize awarded for an outstanding game.

Benko Gambit: p 117.

Bird's Opening: p 118.

Bishop: p 12, etc.

Bishops of opposite colour: p 36.

'Bite on granite': To attack, by means of a piece, an enemy pawn thoroughly well defended by another pawn.

Blind spot of a knight: p 39.

Blindfold chess Chess without sight of a board.

Blitz chess: Very quick games (usually five minutes per player for the whole game).

Block: (a) To deny the use of a square by putting a man on it; (b) A problem in which White cannot mate until Black has weakened his position by moving.

Blockading (a pawn): p 79.

Blocked position: p 37.

Blunder: Disastrous move.

Book (describing play or a move): frequently adopted, familiar.

Bookish (ditto): stereotyped, uninspired.

BPCF: (The) British Postal Chess Federation.

Breakthrough: p 74.

Brevity: Short, decisive game.

Brilliancy: Brilliantly played game.

Brilliancy Prize: A prize given for the most brilliantly-played game in a tournament, irrespective of the winner's total final score.

BUCA: (The) British Universities' Chess Association.

Buchholz (score): Tie-breaking method often used in Swiss System tournaments. A Buchholz score is a player's score multiplied by the sum of his opponents' scores.

Budapest Gambit: p 117.

Cable match: Similar to telephone match. There have been several matches between London and New York, over the cables. Short-wave radio has been similarly utilised over distances up to 6,000 miles, Hollywood once playing Honolulu this way.

Candidates' cycle: Elimination series to decide who will challenge the world champion.

Capture: p 13.

Caro-Kann Defence: p 116.

Castle: Old name for rook.

Castle long (to): To castle on the queenside ('0-0-0').

Castle short (to): To castle on the kingside ('0-0').

Castling: pp 24-25.

Casual game: Non-competitive contest.

'Caterpillar display': A simultaneous display in which two strong players take on a number of weaker players, each of the strong players making alternate moves in each game.

Centre-Counter Game: p 116.

Centre Game: The opening 1 e4 e5 2 d4. Weak; after 2 ... exd4 3 ♛xd4 White's queen becoming an object of attack.

Change-mate: p 127.

Chatauranga: Indian parent game of chess.

Check: pp 13-14.

Checkmate: pp 9, 25-26.

Chess clock: p 51.

Chess Festival: Gatherings of chess players which were organised by the author of this book annually for many years.

CHESS Monthly: Popular monthly magazine. For further details write to Chess and Bridge Ltd, 369 Euston Road, London NW1 3AR.

Closed game: One in which the pieces are developed behind the pawns and come only slowly into contact with each other.

Colle System (of opening): White plays d2-d4, e2-e3, c2-c3 (if necessary), ♗d3, ♘bd2, ♘gf3, 0-0 and ♕c2, then breaks open the position with e2-e4 at the favourable moment, with a view to a direct kingside attack. Simple but quite strong.

Combination: A series of moves serving one specific aim.

Command: A square is 'commanded' when a hostile man occupying it might be captured. There is an alternative stronger meaning, favoured by Continental writers: that no enemy man would dare to move on to that square.

Compensation: Advantages that may offset those of the opponent.

Connected pawn: A pawn that may guard or be guarded by another on an adjacent file.

Cook: p 126.

Correspondence chess: Chess by post.

Counter-gambit: p 118.

Counter-sacrifice: When a player has sacrificed material for position: sacrifice in return by his opponent of material to finish with an overall advantage - even perhaps only a small superiority in position. A powerful weapon in foiling an attack.

Cramped: Restricted in space or movement.

Cross-check: In answering a check by interposing, a player himself delivers check. One or both checks may be 'discovered'.

Danish Gambit: 1 e4 e5 2 d4 exd4 3 c3. Black refutes by capturing pawns as offered and then immediately counter-sacrificing a pawn by ... d7-d5.

Defaults: If a player retires from an all-play-all tournament (e.g. through illness).

(a) Before completing half his games, all his results should be annulled.

(b) After completing half his games, his score should stand and his remaining games be scored to his opponents by default.

In postal chess, if such a defaulter has made some moves against all other participants in the event, his unfinished games should be adjudicated.

Defence: (a) An opening characterised by a move by Black; (b) Operations against an opponent who holds the initiative.

Defend: Same as 'protect' or 'guard'. (Special) conduct a defence.

Descriptive notation: A system of notation that was popular in English-speaking countries until the 1970s. Nowadays nearly all books and periodicals appear in algebraic notation.

Develop: To bring out a piece; to move it from its original position to one more favourable for attack or defence.

Diagonal: p 22.

Discovered attack: p 29.

Discovered check: p 29.

Dissolved doubled pawns: The elimination of a doubled pawn by exchanging.

Distant passed pawn: p 85.

Divergent attack or Double attack: p 56.

Double check: p 29

Doubled pawns: p 77.

Doubled rooks: p 42.

Draw, Drawn game: p 20.

Dual: Choice of mating moves. A blemish.

Duress: p 127.

Dutch Defence: p 117.

ECO: *Encyclopaedia of Chess Openings.*

Eighth rank: The rank furthest from a player, his pawns reaching which can be 'promoted' (Diagram 20).

Elo rating: System of rating chess players used by FIDE and many national bodies.

Empress: A piece in 'fairy chess' combining the powers of rook and knight.

Encyclopaedia of Chess Openings: Comprehensive survey of all known chess openings.

Endgame, Ending: p 44.

Endgame study: see Study.

English Opening: p 117.

'En passant': p 18.

'En prise': p 10.

Escape hole (for king): p 27.

Establish (a piece or pawn): To place it in a position from which it cannot profitably be dislodged.

Evans Gambit: 1 e4 e5 2 ♘f3 ♘c6 3 ♗c5 ♗c5 4 b4. Probably sound - certainly lively.

Exchanging: p 102.

Exchange, To win the: To win a rook for bishop or knight.

Fairy chess: An extension of problem chess into the realms of fantasy, to include all types of boards, men, playing conditions and aims of play.

Falkbeer Counter-gambit: 1 e4 e5 2 f4 d5. Quite good.

Family fork: Humorous name given by Bogolyubov to the fork by a knight simultaneously of several enemy pieces at once, especially king, queen and rook.

Fianchetto: Development of a bishop on g2 (g7) after g2-g3 (g7-g6) or b2 (b7) after b2-b3 (b7-b6).

Fianchettoed: So developed.

FIDE: The International Chess Federation (Federation Internationale des Echecs), a body founded in 1924. From 1948 until the formation of the PCA in 1993 FIDE exclusively administered the world championship.

FIDE master: Internationally recognised title below grandmaster and international master.

FIDE rating: International rating based on system developed by Arpad Elo.

File: p 21.

Finger-slip: Picking up another man than that intended.

Flag (of chess clock): p 51.

Flank: see Side.

Flight, Flight square: Square to which a king is free to move.

Fool's mate: The mate given on p 107.

Forced move: The one move which can be made without immediate disaster.

Fork: p 56.

Fortress: An unassailable stronghold that results in a drawn game.

Four-handed chess: Pairs of partners play, seated as at whist, on a special large board. Each has a full set of men. A player mated can come back into the game if his partner relieves the mate.

Four Knights Opening: p 116.

French Defence: p 116.

From Gambit: p 118.

Gambit: p 116.

Giuoco Piano: p 115.

Good bishop: p 90.

Grading system: Method of classifying players.

Grandmaster: A higher rank than 'international master' with qualification requirements similarly defined.

Grandmaster draw: Short draw without a fight.

Grasshopper: A fairy chess piece moving in the same directions as a queen, but only by jumping over a piece (of either colour) to the next square beyond.

Greco Counter-gambit: p 116.

Grünfeld Defence: p 117.

Guarding: p 45.

Half-open file: A file containing no friendly pawns but one or more hostile pawns.

Half-pin: p 69.

Handicapping: See Odds.

Hanging pawns: United pawns (especially when on the 4th, 5th or 6th ranks) without companions on either adjacent file.

Heavy piece: p 39.

Helpmate: A problem in which White and Black conspire together to play the one series of moves leading to a mate.

Hole: p 82.

Horrwitz bishops: Two fellow bishops on neighbouring diagonals (as in Diagram 35) (named after a player famous for exploiting their power).

Hypermodern: School of chess that developed in the 1920s. The Nimzo-Indian Defence and King's Indian Defence are two hypermodern openings.

Illegal: Against the laws of chess.

Indian Defence: A defence in which Black develops his king's knight before centre pawns, the latter being held back for a few moves, until their best stations become evident. Often involves fianchettoing at least one bishop.

Informator (Chess Informant): Thrice yearly survey of the best games of the preceding months.

Initiative: The ability to shape the subsequent course of the game to one's choice, more or less.

Interference: A man, in moving for some purpose, hinders the effectiveness of a fellow-man in some way.

Intermediate move: A move which takes the place of, and postpones for one turn, an inevitable move such as a recapture (also known as a *zwischenzug*).

Interposing: p 14.

International master: Title awarded by FIDE for outstanding results in international tournaments; one step below Grandmaster.

Interpose: Move a piece so that it interferes with the action of an opposing piece along a file, rank or diagonal.

Interzonal tournament: Qualification tournament to decide who will go forward into the Candidates' cycle.

Inversion of moves, To invert moves: Same as transposition,

transpose.
Isolani: An isolated pawn.
Isolated pawn: p 76.
'J'adoube': p 50.
'Jamboree': A system by which several teams can meet, and their relative scores be determined after only one game by each player. Each team's opponents are drawn as equally as possible from all the other teams. Thus with four teams, A, B, C, D, of six players each, A's strongest player might meet B's strongest, A's second player might meet C's second; A's third might meet D's third; A's fourth, B's fourth, and so on. Each player has one game, then the team's score is totted up ... and that is all!
Key, key-move: p 123.
'Kibitzer': Spectator prone to offering persistent advice.
King: p 11, etc.
King's field: the squares to which a king could legally move, assuming no other men were on the board.
King's Gambit: pp 116, 118.
King's Indian Defence: p 117.
Knight: p 12, etc.
'Kriegspiel': An amusing offshoot of chess in which each player is kept in ignorance of the positions of his opponent's men, apart from such information as he can glean, e.g. from his king not being permitted to move on to a certain square. Each plays with a board and men of his own; only the umpire, sitting between them with a third board and men, can

see more than one board and play the actual complete game.
Knock-out Tournament: A tournament in which any competitor losing a game is 'knocked out' from the contest.
'Ladder' competition: A continuous contest in which successes bring ascents in a vertical list of names of contestants; often hung up in a club room.
Lightning chess: p 53.
'Little combination': Capablanca's half humorous term for a simple operation (e.g. giving away a piece to recover it next move) securing a slight improvement in position.
Living chess: Actors robed as chess pieces move on squares marked out on a level patch of ground. Attractive pageantry.
Long diagonal: (In Kriegspiel) the longer of the two diagonals on which a king receives check. (In ordinary chess) one of the diagonals from corner to corner of the board.
'Lopez grip': The sustained positional advantage gained by White in the Ruy Lopez opening (sometimes called 'Spanish torture).
'Lust to expand': Nimzowitsch's term for the tendency of a pawn to advance and, in doing so, increase in power.
Major piece: p 39.
Man: p 9.
Manufacturing a fork, pin etc.: p 61, etc.
Maroczy Bind: p 119.

Master: Strong player.
Match: A competition between two players, or between two teams of players. In the latter case, it should be obligatory on each team to list their players in order of playing strength so that the strongest player on each side meets the strongest on the other, and so on.
Mate: pp 9, 25-26.
Mating net: Commanding of most of the squares in a king's field by two or more hostile pieces, so that mate can be threatened, usually in more than one way.
Material: Very general term for amount of chessmen.
Max Lange Attack: A complicated and artificial variation of the Giuoco Piano.
MCO: *Modern Chess Openings.*
Meredith: A problem with between 8 and 12 pieces.
Middlegame: The portion of the game between the opening and the endgame; vaguely, it starts when all the pieces have been developed, ends when enough pieces have been exchanged away to permit the kings safely to become active.
Miniature: (In problems) a problem with seven pieces or fewer. (In standard play) a short, decisive game.
Minor exchange, The: Bishop for knight.
Minor piece: A bishop or knight.
Mobile formation of pawns: p 75.

Mobility: p 98.
Model Mate: A 'pure' mate in which every attacking man is utilised. Pretty!
Modern Benoni Defence: p 117.
Modern Chess Openings: Famous encyclopaedia of the openings, which has run through many editions.
Modern Defence p 116.
Movebound: p 127.
Mutate: p 127.
Nightriders: A fairy chess piece moving in straight lines (just like a rook or bishop) but along lines of squares a knight's move apart, e.g. from a1 to e3 or g4.
Nimzo-Indian Defence: pp 117, 120.
Noah's Ark Trap: p 120.
Notation: See Chapter 9.
Odds: An initial advantage conceded by a stronger player to a weaker. A common scale of odds is:

(a) Pawn and move. The player conceding the odds take (unless another pawn is specified) his f-pawn off the board to start with and his opponent has first move.

(b) Pawn and two moves. The odds-giver takes off his f-pawn and his opponent makes two moves before he moves at all.

(c) Knight (the odds giver starts a knight short).

(d) Rook.

(e) Two minor pieces.

Other methods of handicapping are:

(1) The stronger player is compelled to mate his opponent

within a given number of moves to score a win, within another specified number to score a draw, otherwise, whatever the position reached, he is scored a loss.

(2) Playing with clocks, the weaker player is given a more generous time-allowance.

(3) A win gains more points for a weaker player than a strong, and similarly in the case of a draw.

(4) An amusing suggestion is that the weaker player might be conceded the right to 'have a move back' in the course of the game (or two moves if the disparity in playing strength is great) after seeing his opponent's reply.

It keeps up interest to vary the method of odds-giving in a club from season to season.

Odds of the draw: The stronger player scores a draw as a loss to him.

Olympiad: Teams of four and two reserves, representing national federations, compete in an event organised by FIDE for a trophy presented by the Hon. F G Hamilton-Russell. At Buenos Aires, in 1939, 28 nations competed, including Britain, Canada, Ireland, France, Poland, Germany, Argentina, Brazil, Norway, Sweden, Holland, Denmark, etc,. etc. By 1992, at Manila, the competing nations had risen to 102. The USSR had been the most frequent winners, and the Russian team continued this success at Manila, with a team that included world champion Garry Kasparov and rising star Vladimir Kramnik.

'One pawn holding two': p 81.

Open diagonal: A diagonal unobstructed by one's own pawns and therefore offering good scope for the action of a queen or bishop (note analogy with Open file).

Open file: p 41.

Open game: One in which the pawns play little part, piece-play predominating.

Opening: (Strictly) As far as mathematical investigations can go. Further in well-known than in bizarre lines of play; at most 15 to 20 moves except in rare cases.

Opposite-coloured bishops: Bishops operating an different coloured diagonals.

Opposition: p 108.

Options: p 99.

Orthodox Defence to Queen's Gambit: p 115, 117.

OTB: Short for over-the-board.

Outpost: A well-defended piece, well advanced.

Over-the-board: Normal play with opponent present, as distinct from postal chess or private analysis.

Over-burdened man: p 70.

Over-loaded: Same as over-burdened.

Passed pawn: p 79.

Patzer: Poor player.

Pawn: p 11, etc.

Pawn majority: p 86.

Pawn-roller: p 75.

Pawn-skeleton: p 82.

Pawn-snatcher: A player inclined to capture pawns to the detriment of his general position.

Pawn-storm: The advancing of a pawn-roller.

PCL: Postal Chess League, a competition inaugurated in 1944, by the author of this book, in which teams of ten from all parts of the British Isles competed in correspondence play.

Perpetual check: p 20.

Petroff Defence: p 116.

Phalanx: A group of connected pawns.

Piece: Strictly, any man but a pawn. Often loosely used for any man.

Pin, pinned, pinning: p 63.

'Ping-pong': p 54.

'Pion coiffe' (Literally 'capped pawn'): An amusing method of giving odds when an expert is playing a novice. The former marks one of his pawns and undertakes to give mate with that pawn (without promoting it). If the 'capped pawn' is captured, or if mate is delivered by any other man, the expert is adjudged to have lost.

Pirc Defence: p 116.

Pocket set: A wallet, usually of leather or plastic, containing a miniature chess board of leather or linen. The men are of bone or celluloid material, appropriately printed or embossed, and slip in and out of slots at the bases of the squares. Games can be played or positions examined in a train, ship, or in fact, almost anywhere.

Polish Defence: 1 d4 b5. Very weak.

Ponziani's Opening: 1 e4 e5 2 c3. Innocuous.

Position: The arrangement of the men at any stage in a game. A player is said to have a good position when his forces have free scope for action and are well-placed for attack and defence.

Positional play: Manoeuvring rather than combinative play.

Positional sacrifice: A sacrifice for compensation in the form not of a quick combinative gain but of subtle, long-term advantages in general manoeuvrability.

Postal chess: Same as correspondence chess.

Postal Chess League: (See PCL).

Post-mortem analysis: After game discussion by the two players.

Power: p 97.

Prepared variation: A variation in the opening, privately analysed before the game and introduced as a surprise departure from 'book' moves.

Pressure: A vague term indicating, e.g. a long-sustained attack against (usually) a pawn, which causes difficulty through the tying down of pieces to its defence.

Princess: A fairy chess piece combing the powers of bishop and knight.

Problems: p 123.

PCA: Professional Chess Association. Body for professional players founded in 1993 by Garry Kasparov and Nigel Short. Kasparov is the current PCA world champion.

Promotion: p 11.

Prophylaxis: Term coined by Nimzowitsch for moves that anticipate an opponent's threats.

Protected passed pawn: A passed pawn protected by another pawn.

'Pure' mate: A mate position in which each square in the mated king's field is only singly guarded or blocked as in Diagram 13.

Quality, The: p 39.

Queen: p 11, etc.

Queening: p 11.

Queening square (of a pawn): p 11.

Queen's Gambit: A game opened by 1 d4 d5 2 c4.

Queen's Gambit Accepted: pp 117, 119.

Queen's Gambit Declined: pp 115, 117.

Queen's Indian Defence: p 117.

Queen's Pawn Game: In general a game opened by 1 d4 but which is not a Queen's Gambit.

Queenside majority: Same as **Queenside pawn majority:** p 86.

Quickplay finish: Speed finish (typically fifteen minutes for each player for the rest of the game) to a game after the first time control.

Radio matches: Around 1946, the resumption of peace was celebrated by radio matches (on the lines of telephone matches or cable matches, which see): USA-USSR, UK-USSR, France- Aus-tralia, Spain-Argentina, etc. There were also some interesting personal matches, e.g., between Barda Norway and Fairhurst Scotland, with the moves announced each evening over the respective national broadcasting programmes so that millions of listeners could follow the games. With the intensification of international contacts, such use of radio has lessened.

Rank: p 21.

'Ranking' or 'Rating' List: Using an arbitrary mathematical formula, the players of a region are listed in order of strength based on the results of all their games over a period.

Rapid chess: Increasingly popular form of chess for one-day tournaments. Each player is usually allocated 30 or 40 minutes for the whole game.

Rapid Transit: American term for blitz or lightning chess p 54.

Recapture: Capture a man that has just captured.

Remote passed pawn: p 85.

Resign: Concede the game (usually in a hopeless situation).

Réti's Opening: p 117.

Retirements: (from a tournament) see Defaults.

Retractor: Problem in which one or more moves are to be taken back before the one line of play leading to mate is sought.

Retrograde Analysis: Detective work to find out the moves by which a given position was reached.

Rook: p 11, etc.

Round Robin (tournament): Same as American or all-play-all.

Ruy Lopez: pp 115, 116.

Sacrifice: To give up material deliberately, calculating to obtain some advantage in position, e.g. see p 128.

Safe pawn grouping: p 75.

Saint George chessmen: An older pattern of man than Staunton, more top heavy and liable to the obscuring of one man by another during play.

'Sans voir': Chess *sans voir* is blindfold chess.

Scholar's mate: The mate given on p 107.

Score sheets: p 107.

Scotch Opening: p 116.

Sealed move, Sealing a move: p 54.

Second: A player's assistant during a match or tournament who will help prepare opening lines and analyse adjourned positions.

Second rank (a player's): the rank on which his pawns start the game.

Self-block: a black man, endeavouring to forestall one mate, moves to a square next to the black king and, by robbing the latter of a flight-square, allows a new mate.

Self-interference: A 'shut-off' (which see) due to interposition by a man of the same colour.

Self-mate: A peculiar type of problem in which White forces his opponent to mate him and

Black strives to avoid doing so.

'Set' mates: Mating variations existing in the original position, e.g., 'if Black moves so-and-so, White mates so-and-so' (p 127).

Seventh rank (a player's): The rank on which his opponent's pawns start the game, p 41.

Shut-off: Interposition by a hostile man which destroys the command by a piece of a square, rank, file, or diagonal.

Sicilian Defence: pp 116, 118-119.

Side (queen's or king's): p 24.

Simplify: Exchange pawns or pieces so as not to gain or lose any men but to clarify the situation.

Simultaneous display: An expert encounters several weaker players, seated at boards which he visits cyclically to make his moves. If his opponents number twenty, he plays twenty games while they play one, and has on average one-twentieth as much time per move.

Simultaneous blindfold display: A simultaneous display in which the expert sees no board or men but is merely told his opponent's moves (made on boards before them) and has to imagine the constantly changing positions in the various games throughout. Alekhine took on 32 really strong opponents in this way at Chicago in 1933, Koltanowski took on 34 in Edinburgh in 1937, Najdorf 45 at Sao Paulo in 1947. Irregularities in the last display and weak

opposition in Koltanowski's make Alekhine's the greatest feat.
Sitzfleisch (A German word meaning 'flesh of the posterior'): Ability to win games through remaining solidly in one's seat hour after hour, making a succession of uninspired but fairly sound moves until one's opponent blunders through boredom.
Skewer: p 63.
Slav Defence to Queen's Gambit: p 117.
Smothered mate: p 31.
Sonneborn-Berger: A method (named after its inventors) of resolving ties in American tournaments. To a player's ordinary score are added, to form his Sonneborn-Berger score, the ordinary score of each opponent he beat in the tournament, and half the ordinary score of each opponent with whom he drew.
Spanish Opening: Another name for the Ruy Lopez.
Speed chess: A loose term for games played at an accelerated time-limit.
Spite check: A check given when the player might well resign, just to prolong the game by one move.
Stalemate: pp 20, 26.
Staunton men: p 10.
Stonewall: An opening (defence or attack) characterised by advance of adjacent pawns alternately to the third and fourth ranks (from the resemblance of the formation to the top of a stone wall).

Study: Rather like a problem but the task is to win or draw, not in any specified number of moves.
Support: Same as protect.
Swindle: Derogatory name for a game positionally lost but won or drawn through a 'trap' or combination which the sufferer could easily have avoided.
Switchback: A piece moving and then returning to its original square.
Swiss system: Participants in a knock-out tournament drop out after one perhaps chancy loss; and an all-play-all requires as many rounds (less one) as there are players. The Swiss system provides a winner (though not necessarily many other reliable placings) from among a large number of players in a few rounds and keeps everybody playing until the end. First-round pairings are decided by lot or seeding. For each subsequent round, each contestant is paired against an opponent who has as nearly as possible the same score as he (nobody meeting the same opposition twice on any account). As far as practicable each player is alternated as White and Black. The pairings for any particular round can be made only when the previous rounds' games have been decided. Very protracted games may have to be adjudicated or decided by quickplay finish.
'Synthetic': An amusing reversal of the normal chess problem. The

solution is given, with or without certain other details, and the solver is asked to construct the original position.

Take: Same as capture.

'Tandem' display: Same as Caterpillar.

Task problem: A problem in which the composer has set out to illustrate some extreme idea.

Technical win: A win which can be obtained from a given position by solid sound play involving no 'brilliancy' or uncertainty.

Telephone match: Two clubs in distant towns book a telephone connection for four hours or so, during which time up to 500 moves can be transmitted each way. Each team should have one personal representative in the other camp. Cheaper than travelling for 100 miles or more but there is a sacrifice of sociableness.

Tempo: A move, or turn to play, considered as a unit of time. Thus 'to lose a tempo' is to make a useless move.

Terrain: Area of board.

Text (The), Text-move: (In commentary on a game): the last move actually played.

Theoretical novelty (TN): A move in the opening which is thought not to have been played before.

Theory: Consensus of opinion (usually on openings) as revealed in the literature.

Threat Problem: One in which White's first move threatens mate and the play revolves around Black's efforts to avert this mate allowing others.

Three-dimensional chess: Chess played inside a cube of some transparent material such as perspex, with eight ordinary boards one above another. The pieces not only move about the individual boards but zoom from board to board. Brain wracking.

Three Knights Opening: p 116.

Three-mover: A 'mate in three moves' problem.

Time Control: Limit on time for each player (typically 40 moves in 2 hours each for international competition).

Time-trouble: Occurs when one or both players has very little time to play the necessary moves to reach the time control.

TN: Theoretical Novelty.

Touch and move: p 49.

Tournament: A competition involving a number of teams or players in which each usually plays every other; 'knock-out' contests being rather unpopular in chess.

Transposition of moves: Reversing the order of successive moves. Hence 'to transpose' moves, e.g. play 1 ♘f3 and 2 e4 instead of 1 e4 and 2 ♘f3.

Trap (to ...): Attack a piece, all of whose squares of possible escape are commanded.

Traps: p 120-121.

Tripled pawns: Three fellow pawns on the same file. A profound weakness.

Try: p 126.

Two bishops (the): p 40.

Two Knights Defence: 1 e4 e5 2 ♘f3 ♘c6 3 ♗c4 ♘f6. Sound. By 4 ♘g5, White can force ... d7-d5 (which sacrifices a pawn; but the sacrifice is generally considered justified).

Two-mover: a 'mate in two moves' problem.

Underpromotion: Promotion of a pawn to a piece other than a queen.

United pawns: Fellow pawns on adjacent files.

Unguarded, unprotected, unsupported: Liable to be captured without possibility of recapture of the capturing man.

'Unlike' Bishops: Same as 'bishops of opposite colour'.

Unpin: To free a pinned piece by interposing; see e.g. p 99.

USCF: United States Chess Federation, the official US body. Americans wishing to contact their national body should write to USCF, 186 Route 9W, New Windsor, NY 12553.

Variation: A series of moves, alternately by White and Black, conditioned by the first.

Vienna Opening: pp 115-116.

Waiter, Waiting Problem: pp 126-127.

Weaknesses: p 81.

Weaver Adams' method: p 81.

Wing (as 'King's wing' or 'Queen's wing'): Same as Side.

Winning the exchange: p 39.

Wood-chopping: Exchanging off men in an uninspired way.

Wood-shifting: Deadly dull chess.

World Championship: p 138.

X-ray attack: Same as 'skewer'.

X-ray check: a check which, if the checked king moves, allows a man behind it to be captured.

Zonal tournament: Preliminary event to decide who will compete in an Interzonal tournament.

Zugzwang: p 127-128.

Zwischenzug: German for intermediate (in-between) move.